Best Family Adventures:
San Luis Obispo County

IMPORTANT LEGAL NOTICE AND DISCLAIMER

Many activities listed, described or otherwise implied in this book are potentially dangerous. Users of this book should take necessary precautions to protect themselves and their families if they choose to participate in any of the activities listed or implied by this publication.

All information in this book is subject to change, including but not limited to locations, contact information, prices and hours of operation. Call ahead for most current information including closures, price changes, new location and rules that may affect the use of any given facility.

The author, editors, contributors, publishers and distributors accept no liability for any errors or omissions in this book or for any injuries or losses incurred while using this book as a resource.

Pen & Pad Publishing
P.O. Box 2995
Orcutt, CA 93457
(805) 938-1307
www.bestfamilyadventures.com
outdoor411@aol.com

Best Family Adventures: San Luis Obispo County
Text and Photos Copyright © 2006 Jennifer Best
All rights reserved.

Printed in the United States of America

ISBN-10   0-9769050-1-9
ISBN-13   978-0-9769050-1-1

Library of Congress Control Number: 2006902986

Researchers: Jennifer Best, Erica Best, Valerie Best, Stephen Best
Editors: Lynn Peterson Price, Julia Cabreros, Susan Degner
Design: Jennifer Best

Acknowledgements

Thank you to all of those who supported this effort from infancy through final distribution. This project could not have been completed without the support of my husband, Steve Best. All research was made possible by our daughters, Erica and Valerie Best, who researched almost every entry in this book with me. Much of the research was also completed with the help of Julia Cabreros. I thank my dad, Randy Peterson, for instilling in me a spirit of adventure, my mom, Lynn Peterson Price, for fully supporting my writing career, and my other mom, Kathy Peterson, for fostering a sense of curiosity.

For Valerie and Erica
May you always keep your sense of adventure

Contents

(Resource section includes reference books, chambers of commerce, parks & rec departments, farmers' markets, public transit, arts associations, music associations, theatrical organizations, and clubs, groups and other gatherings)

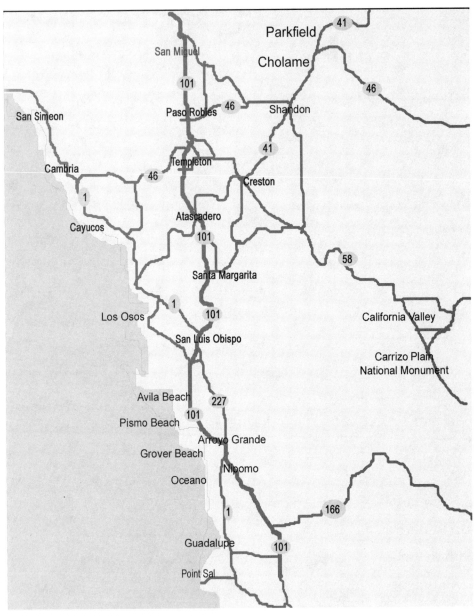

SAN LUIS OBISPO COUNTY

Throughout this book you will see price ranges. All prices are subject to change. At press time the following applied:

FREE! = FREE!

$ = $10 or less per person

$$ = $11-$20 per person

$$$ = $21 or more per person

☛ indicates Best Bets when time's too short to hit them all

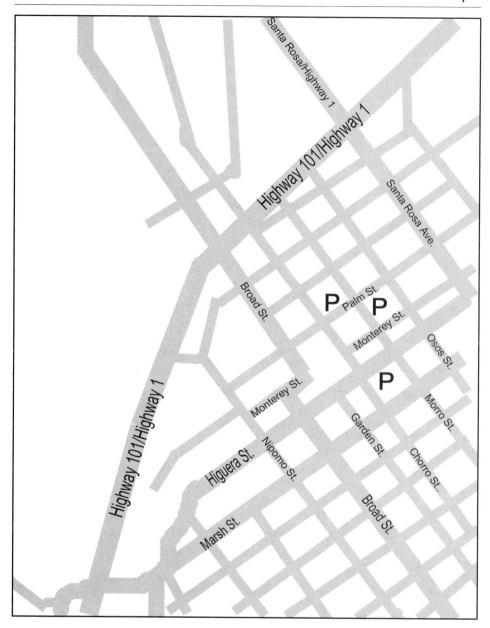

DOWNTOWN SAN LUIS OBISPO

Parking can be a challenge. The easiest solution is to head to the parking structures (**P**) at Marsh and Chorro Streets, Palm Street east of Chorro Street, and Palm Street east of Morro Street. The first hour is free.

POLY CANYON offers a variety of trails for hikers, mountain bikers and equestrian use. The Design Village offers a unique opportunity to view student architectural efforts up close. Ridge trails offer splendid views. Opportunities for birding, wildflower viewing and creek play abound.

Chapter 1

San Luis Obispo

San Luis Obispo is haven for families with children of any age. The county seat and namesake boasts a chain of 65-million-year-old volcanic peaks, rolling hills, meandering creeks, arts opportunities, parks as well as a variety of eateries and activities designed specifically with children in mind.

It is little wonder so many people have made this temperate valley home. The centrally located city within a few minutes' drive of beaches, lakes and mountains was home to the Chumash people for centuries before Mission San Luis Obispo de Tolosa was established here in 1772. The fifth of the state's original 21 missions remains the focal point downtown. Services are still held in the chapel, festivals are celebrated in the plaza, children continue throwing rocks across the creek while the smells of good food and sounds of live music float through the fresh air.

San Luis Obispo is home to 30 parks including pocket parks locals may hardly notice and sports complexes that play home to tournaments throughout the year. Many of the larger parks have group areas available by reservation.

On-street parking in downtown San Luis Obispo is metered and often hard to find, but the city provides ample parking in a number of centrally located parking garages where the first hour is free: on Marsh Street at Chorro Street; on Palm Street between Chorro and Morro streets; or off Palm Street at Morro Street.

The city is also home to California Polytechnic State University (Cal Poly).

ARTS

ASI Craft Center Gallery
First Floor of Julian McPhee University Union, Cal Poly
(805) 756-1266
www.asi.calpoly.edu/uu/craftcenter
FREE!-$$$
From Highway 101, take the Grand Avenue exit north onto the Cal Poly campus. Stop at the information booth on the right side of the road immediately upon entering campus for a parking pass. Continue onto campus. The gallery is inside the student union at the intersection of Perimeter Road and Grand Avenue.

This art center and gallery features student works and public workshops, special sales and an annual Throwfest, a 24-hour clay throwing event held each February. The gallery is generally open Sunday through Wednesday from noon to 6 p.m., though hours vary. Call ahead.

The gallery often shows works of ceramic, clay, stained glass, blown glass and photography. The center offers public art classes at $70 per student or public workshops at $3 per person per craft project. Workshops can include candle dipping, tie dye, hemp projects, soap making, clay work and stained glass. Workshops vary to fit participants' ages. Call for workshop reservations or class schedule.

Boo Boo Records Kids Music

978 Monterey St.

(805) 541-0657

www.booboorecords.com

FREE!

From Highway 101, take the Marsh Street exit and continue straight into town. Turn left onto Osos Street then left onto Monterey Street.

Every Wednesday at 10 a.m. babies and toddlers crowd into the record store's back room to dance, wiggle and drum to their little hearts' content. Music changes weekly and occasionally there are special guests.

Cal Poly Performing Arts Center

1 Grand Ave.

(805) 756-7222

www.pacslo.org

$$$

From Highway 101 take the Grand Avenue exit and head north onto the Cal Poly Campus. Parking information and passes are available at the booth to the right immediately upon entering campus.

The center includes the Christopher Cohan Center, featuring a world-class, 1,282-seat concert hall. It also houses the 497-seat Cal Poly Theatre, a 170-seat recital hall and a pavilion. Local organizations and professional troupes from around the world take the stage here throughout the year. Check the center's calendar for current offerings.

Rules regarding children are strictly enforced, so beware when purchasing tickets. Babies and children are only allowed when expressly stated in an event's advertising. All children must have a ticket, even if they are small enough to fit on an adult's lap. Any child disrupting a performance will be ushered from the theater along with one guardian and will not be allowed to return to the seating area until intermission.

Downtown Centre Cinemas

888 Marsh St.

(805) 546-8600

$

From Highway 101 take the Marsh Street exit and continue straight into downtown.

While it focuses on playing blockbusters, this theater's unique location underground may give it added interest value. Drop down the big steps to seven screens of escapism.

☛ Fremont Theater

1025 Monterey St.

(805) 541-2141

www.themovieexperience.com/cl-sroom.shtml

$

From Highway 101, take the Marsh Street exit and continue straight into town. Turn left onto Osos Street, then right onto Monterey Street.

To give children a true movie experience, bring them to this Art Deco cinema. The Fremont was built in 1942 and has served generations of movie goers in style with a truly big screen and plenty of comfortable seats for a crowd. Murals of sea nymphs on horseback adorn the interior walls. Other touches include the neon-illuminated swoops on the ceiling, floor-to-ceiling velvet drapes and inlaid walkways.

The theater generally screens blockbusters, but it also features special showings including the ongoing Screening Room Classics series. It is also the featured theater during the San Luis Obispo International Film Festival (www.slofilmfest.org) held annually.

The neighboring Mission Cinemas adds three modern screens to the mix.

Hands Gallery

777 Higuera St.

(805) 543-1921

www.handsgallery.com

FREE!

From Highway 101 take the Marsh Street exit and continue straight into town. Turn left onto Chorro Street, and then left onto Higuera Street. The gallery is on the left.

Local artists and more show their works at this commercial gallery. Kids who can keep their hands to themselves are appreciated in this store full of breakable but intriguing works of art including utilitarian pieces for all ages.

Just Looking Gallery

746 Higuera St., Suite 1

(805) 541-6663

www.justlookinggallery.com

FREE!

From Highway 101 take the Marsh Street exit and continue straight into town. Turn left onto Chorro Street, and then left onto Higuera Street. The gallery is in the Mission Mall on the right.

For more than 20 years this locally owned gallery has offered limited editions, original works and pieces that offer humor, beauty and "serious" art.

☛ Palm Theatre

817 Palm St.

(805) 541-5161

www.thepalmtheatre.com

$$

From southbound Highway 101 take the Chorro Street exit, take the first two rights to get onto Chorro Street, then turn left onto Palm Street. From northbound Highway 101 take the Broad Street exit and continue straight, then turn left onto Palm Street.

This three-screen theater offers everything no other theater in San Luis Obispo County does: the best of cinema. Come here for foreign films, low-budget festival award winners, documentaries and occasional exceptional blockbusters. You'll also find a reasonably priced snackbar and friendly staff.

Public Art

FREE!

The city of San Luis Obispo is home to many galleries and other public art displays and events. Check the SLO Arts Council website (www.sloartscouncil.org) or stop by the San Luis Obispo Art Center (1010 Broad St., 805-543-8562) or San Luis Obispo Chamber of Commerce Visitors Center (1039 Chorro St., 805-781-2777) for current art brochures, maps and events calendars.

San Luis Obispo Art Center

1010 Broad St.

(805) 543-8562

www.sloartcenter.org

☛ FREE!

From Highway 101 take the Marsh Street exit and follow Marsh into town. Turn left onto Broad Street. The center is two blocks up and on the right.

The art center located on the western edge of Mission Plaza features three galleries of fine art and craft exhibits that change regularly. The center specializes in sharing works of local professional and amateur artists. It also offers classes, workshops and its annual Plein Air Festival. Works of member artists are on sale throughout the year. Take a tour led by a friendly docent, or let your children take the lead. Admission is free, but donations are welcomed.

San Luis Obispo Little Theatre

888 Morro St.

(805) 786-2440

www.slolittletheatre.org

$$

From Highway 101 take the Marsh Street exit and follow Marsh into town. Turn left onto Morro Street. The theater is three blocks up and on the right.

This 58-year-old non-profit community theater company promotes non-professional theater through a variety of offerings including: plays, musicals, readers' theater, and classes and workshops for adults and children.

SLO ART Gallery

339 Marsh St.

(805) 542-9000

www.sloart.com

FREE!

From Highway 101 take the Marsh Street exit and continue straight into town. The gallery is in the Frame Works building on the right.

This gallery features framed works by local artists and special guest artists. Shows rotate every three months or so.

LETTERS

San Luis Obispo City/County Library

995 Palm Street

(805) 781-5775 (children's desk)

www.slolibrary.org

FREE!

From Highway 101 take the Marsh Street exit and continue straight into town. Turn left onto Morro Street. The library is at the corner of Morro and Palm streets.

This relatively large library, open Tuesdays through Saturdays, has a long history of excellent story times catering to preschoolers and toddlers. Call for current schedule.

HISTORY

Ah Louis Store

800 Palm Street

www.visitslo.com

FREE!

From Highway 101 take the Broad Street exit. Turn north one block to Chorro Street, then east on Chorro to Palm Street.

The two-story brick structure was the first Chinese store in San Luis Obispo County when it opened in 1874. It served as the hub of San Luis Obispo's Chinatown. Ah Louis sold general merchandise, herbs and Chinese goods. His store also served as a bank, counting house and post office for the Chinese immigrants who dug the eight tunnels through the Santa Lucia Mountain Range from 1884 to 1894.

The store remains in the hands of the Louis family, which operated it as a retail shop for decorative items from China until 2006.

Camp San Luis Historical Museum
5 miles north of San Luis Obispo on Highway 1
(805) 594-6517
www.militarymuseum.org/campsanluisobispo.html
FREE!
From Highway 101, take the Santa Rosa Street/Highway 1 exit and turn north. Continue out of town. Camp San Luis is on the left.

Since the 1920s, Camp San Luis Obispo has been home to the California National Guard. The 223rd Infantry Regiment, among other training and logistic operations and programs, calls the facility home. The grounds also serve as a living memorial and museum. Static displays include an Army aviation display area with fixed and rotary wing aircraft from the 1950s and '60s. The central mall includes various vehicles, examples of sculpture by Italian prisoners of war interned at the camp during World War II, and a Bataan Memorial. There is a small indoor museum to the right shortly after entering the camp. In addition, the camp houses the California Conservation Corps State Museum which documents the history of the *Civilian Conservation Corps* and the present *California Conservation Corps.*

To enter the camp, driver must show proof of insurance, registration and driver's license.

Central Coast Veterans Memorial Museum
Veterans Memorial Hall
801 Grand Ave.
(805) 543-1763
www.vetmuseum.org
FREE!
From Highway 101 take the Grand Avenue exit. Turn south onto Grand Avenue.

Young history buffs in the making may enjoy this museum of war memorabilia including cannons, helmets, uniforms, maps, flags and military patches, among other items. Hours are Wednesdays through Fridays from 10 a.m. to 3 p.m., and Saturdays 10 a.m. to 12:30 p.m.

Civilian Conservation Corps State Museum
1536 Modoc, Camp San Luis
(805) 788-0517
FREE!
From Highway 101, take the Santa Rosa Street/Highway 1 exit and turn north. Continue out of town and pass Camp San Luis. Turn left onto Hollister Avenue/Cuesta College, turn left onto O'Conner Road, turn right onto Madera, and then turn left onto Modoc.

The museum is located in four barracks at Camp San Luis and is open by appointment only. The buildings feature the past, present and future of the corps that was established in 1933 by Pres. Franklin Delano Roosevelt. Roosevelt hoped the corps forestry work would prevent soil erosion, provide flood control and complete other projects as the needs arose, but said the chief focus would be "the moral and spiritual value of such work." A library and research center includes more than 100 binders of letters home, information about works completed, and more.

Dallidet Adobe & Gardens
1185 Pacific St.
(805) 543-6762
www.slochs.org/dallidet/main.html
$

From Highway 101, take the Marsh Street exit and continue straight into town. Turn right onto Santa Rosa Street then left onto Pacific Street.

This historic adobe home, owned since 1953 by the San Luis Obispo County Historical Society, provides a field trip experience back to the 1830s. The furnished home was once home to Pierre Hypolite Dallidet and Ascención Salazar, developers of the first commercial winery on the Central Coast. It has also been named California State Historical Landmark No. 720. The garden is open to the public Thursdays from 2:30 p.m. to 5:30 p.m. Docent-led tours of the adobe are held from 1 p.m. to 4 p.m. Sundays from Memorial Day to Labor Day weekends.

Jack House
536 Marsh Street
(805) 781-7308
www.slocity.org/parksandrecreation
$

From Highway 101 take the Marsh Street exit. The house is on the left about two blocks down.

This historic Victorian house and garden is home to a variety of special events, some of which cater to children. Great spot for children learning about the Victorian era. The garden includes a group barbecue area and there are restrooms on the site. Tours are held from 1 p.m. to 4 p.m. on the first Sundays September through May, with additional hours Thursday from 2 p.m. to 5 p.m. June to August. Children accompanied by adults are admitted free of charge.

Mission San Luis Obispo de Tolosa
Monterey Street between Chorro and Broad streets
(805) 543-6850
www.missionsanluisobispo.org
☛ FREE!

From Highway 101 take the Marsh Street exit. Turn right onto Chorro Street. The mission is on the right midway through the second block.

This historic Catholic mission, the fifth of the 21 missions established in California, was founded in 1772. More than 200 years later it remains the focal point of downtown San Luis Obispo and serves as a great tool for bringing history lessons to life. It has also been named California State Historical Landmark #325. The main chapel, which houses a particularly unique vestibule/bell tower, still houses Catholic church services regularly in addition to special services, concerts and other public events throughout the year. The chapel, mission and gardens are open for public tours daily from 9 a.m. to 4 p.m., and guided tours are held every Sunday at 1:15 p.m. Additional tours for groups are available by reservation. Donation requested.

Octagonal Barn
About 4400 South Higuera Street
FREE!

From Highway 101 take Los Osos Valley Road east, turn right onto South Higuera Street.

Though this barn is on private property, it is an interesting and rare structure clearly visible from the public roadway. Local groups have raised tens of thousands of dollars to restore the barn, which is one of only three of its kind remaining in California.

Ramona Railroad Depot
1011 Railroad Ave.
FREE!

From Highway 101 take the Marsh Street exit. Turn right onto Osos Street and continue straight. Follow the jog to the left at the triangular park, and then turn left (around the roundabout) into the parking lot.

The restored train depot is used daily by Amtrak trains headed north and south. Bring the kids by to watch the big diesels pass, take a trip, or check out old photos in the depot.

San Luis Obispo County Historical Museum

Carnegie Library
696 Monterey St.
(805) 543-0638
www.slochs.org
☛ FREE!

From Highway 101 take the Marsh Street exit and head straight into town. Turn left onto Broad Street, then right onto Monterey Street. The museum is on the left inside the Carnegie Library.

Just a skip across the street from Mission San Luis Obispo is the county's most extensive collection of publicly available historical documents. The building, a Carnegie Library built in 1904/05, served as the city's central library until 1955. The following year the San Luis Obispo County Historical Society entered into a lengthy lease agreement with the city. A retrofit and remodel in 2001 gave rise to an expanded exhibit area and public research room. Today, rotating exhibits feature local history and culture.

San Luis Obispo Railway Museum

Railroad Ave.
(805) 461-3456
www.slorrm.com

From Highway 101 take the Marsh Street exit. Turn right onto Osos Street and continue straight. Follow the jog to the left at the triangular park, and then turn right nto the parking lot.

This museum-in-the-making plans to spotlight the history of the Central Coast's rail systems, including the full-gauge rails still in operation and the narrow gauge rails that made many Central Coast communities what they are today. The museum will collect, restore and display railroad artifacts. Several locomotives and other rolling stock are already on hand.

NATURE

San Luis Obispo City Park Rangers lead monthly hikes through various open spaces. Call (805) 781-7302 for current schedule.

Anholm Park

870 Mission St.
(805) 781-7222
www.slocity.org/parksandrecreation
FREE!

From Highway 101 take the Marsh Street exit and continue straight into town. Turn left onto Chorro Street, then right onto Mission Street.

Less-than-a-quarter-acre pocket park with play structure, picnic table, benches. No restroom.

Bishop Peak Natural Reserve

(805) 781-7300

www.ci.san-luis-obispo.ca.us/parksandrecreation

☛ FREE!

From Highway 101 take Santa Rosa Street north, turn left onto Foothill Boulevard, then right onto Patricia Drive. Turn left onto Highland Drive and follow the cul-de-sac to its end. Parking is limited to space available on the street. If all parking is taken, return to Patricia, turn left, park near Anacapa Court and begin your adventure on the Patricia Street Access which dovetails into the Ferrini trail.

The picturesque 1,559-foot Bishop Peak that dominates the horizon west of San Luis Obispo is one in a chain of nine prominent lava plugs left by volcanoes formed more than 20 million years ago. "The Nine Sisters" or "the morros" stretch from Morro Bay to Edna Valley southeast of San Luis Obispo. They include, from west to east, Morro Rock, Black Hill, Cerro Cabrillo, Hollister Peak, Cerro Romauldo, Chumash Peak, Bishop Peak, Cerro San Luis and Little Islay Hill. All but Morro Rock, Hollister Peak and Chumash Peak are accessible to the public. Access to Cerro Romauldo is controlled by Camp San Luis and is limited to groups with proof of $1 million insurance coverage.

Giant volcanic stones balance precariously atop Bishop Peak which has long since been overcome by soil, grasses, wildflowers, oaks and bay trees. The morro is home to the original Cal Poly "P," a giant, whitewashed letter emblazoned on the rocky mountainside by enthusiastic students of yesteryear. The mountain also was home to a granite quarry that supplied the stones for the historic Presbyterian Church at the corner of Marsh and Morro streets in downtown San Luis Obispo. The quarry has long been defunct and decades of winter storms and summer sunshine have faded the old "P," but the peak remains a popular destination for local hikers and rock climbers.

A fairly fit adult carrying a toddler in a pack can make the 2-mile trip to the peak in 1½ hours, which includes stops to watch deer, butterflies and plentiful lizards. The walk down takes about 45 minutes with no stops. The hike is strenuous, rocky and the trails do not provide access for people in wheelchairs or of limited physical capacity. There are no services. Bring plenty of water and snacks, and carry out whatever you carry in.

There are other, more family-friendly options in the reserve including Felsman's Loop. This 2.7-mile hike meanders along the morro's northwestern foothill.

Other important facts: no fires, overnight camping, or bicycles are allowed. Dogs must be on leash. Hikers are asked to stay on trails.

Buena Vista Park
Buena Vista Avenue between Hope and McCollum streets
(805) 781-7300
www.slocity.org/parksandrecreation
FREE!

From Highway 101 take the Grand Avenue exit. Head north, turn right onto Loomis Street then left onto Buena Vista Avenue.

Nearly ½ acre pocket park in something akin to a roundabout.

Cal Poly animal units
(805) 756-2419
www.calpoly.edu
☞ FREE!

From Highway 101, take the Grand Avenue exit north onto the Cal Poly campus, stopping for a parking pass at the information booth immediately on your right upon entering campus.

Cal Poly's learn-by-doing spirit extends to visitors at its various animal units which are open for public tours during daylight hours. Children who ask questions of students at work are likely to find the answers for themselves through hands-on experience.

Swine unit
From the information booth at Grand Avenue, take Grand Avenue north, turn right onto Perimeter Road, turn right onto Via Carta then left onto Sports Complex Road.

Breeder hogs kept outside are friendly and welcome pats and scratches from visitors. While children may be aware of the oinks and snorts hogs are known for making, give these beasts a good scratch between the shoulder blades for a new sound experience. The area also includes a farrowing barn that is sometimes available for tours and a shoat barn.

Dairy Unit
From the information booth at Grand Avenue, take Grand Avenue north, turn right onto Perimeter Road, right onto Via Carta, left onto Highland Drive, then right onto Mt. Bishop Road.

Check out the milking barn and hundreds of dairy cows at this facility. Calves are sometimes available for petting here, too.

Horse Unit
From the information booth at Grand Avenue, take Grand Avenue north, turn right onto Perimeter Road, turn right onto Via Carta and follow it to its end at the horse unit.

The breeding and training facility managed by students is home to plenty of friendly mares itching for a scratch. Watch little ones' fingers which horses could easily mistake for scrumptious carrots or other favorite treats. (But please don't feed the animals.)

Cal Poly Farm Hike

polyland.calpoly.edu/topics/recreation/x330/Polymountainmap.htm
FREE!
From Highway 101 turn north onto Highway 1, right onto Highland Drive, left onto Mount Bishop Road and park in the Crop Unit parking lot.

Cal Poly encourages hiking throughout its lands. Just remember to leave gates as you found them.

This easy hike meanders past several agricultural units including the beef unit, experimental farm, dairy and poultry units. From the parking lot walk west to Stenner Creek then follow the dirt road north along the creek past the orchards, lagoon and Parker Ranch. Turn left onto the paved road (Mount Bishop Road) and continue past the beef unit. After the beef unit turn right onto Stenner Creek Road, then circle the poultry unit. Just north of the poultry unit is an intersection with an unnamed dirt road. Take the trail at the south east corner and continue through the open grassland and onto a dirt road that leads past the organic experimental farm, south to the dairy unit then back to Mount Bishop Road and, eventually, the car.

Cal Poly Plant Shop

(805) 756-1106
www.calpoly.edu
FREE!
From Highway 101, take the Grand Avenue exit north onto the Cal Poly campus, stopping for a parking pass at the information booth immediately upon entering campus. Continue along Grand Avenue, turn right onto Perimeter Road, and turn right onto Via Carta. The plant shop and greenhouse are on the right directly across from the horse stables.

Student-grown plants of many varieties are on display and for sale here. Bring a picnic and enjoy the tree-shaded lawn and deck that separates the greenhouse from the equine unit. Bring some cash to pick up seasonal flowers and other plants started here.

Cal Poly U-pick

(805) 756-2224
www.calpoly.edu
$-$$$
From Highway 101, take the Grand Avenue exit north onto the Cal Poly campus, stopping for a parking pass at the information booth immediately upon entering campus. Crop locations vary. Call ahead for specific directions.

Cal Poly students lead this enterprising effort to share the crops they grow. The public is welcome to take part picking whatever crop is in season including stonefruits, citrus and pumpkins Wednesdays from 2 p.m. to 5 p.m. and Saturdays from 10 a.m. to 1 p.m. School and other group tours of the pumpkin patch are available in the fall when a corn maze is also open. Pumpkin picking is available late in the pumpkin season.

Cerro San Luis Natural Reserve
(805) 781-7300
www.slocity.org/parksandrecreation
☛ FREE!

From San Luis Obispo, take Marsh Street west toward southbound Highway 101. After crossing under the freeway, take an immediate right onto Fernandez Road (the last right before entering the highway).

This 118-acre reserve has long been a primary public access to Cerro San Luis, one of the city's signature peaks complete with its historic "M" commemorating Mission Preparatory High School in San Luis Obispo. Trails in the reserve vary, but all involve a climb. Sites include outcroppings of cactus that protect a variety of plant species seldom seen elsewhere in the city, an old lemon grove, and access to the "M."

The hike to the peak is fairly strenuous in that it involves a continuous uphill walk, but, due to the relatively clear path and graded incline, it is regularly traveled by people of all ages and physical abilities. This is also an excellent mountain bike ride with wide paths that accommodate both bikers and hikers.

Another public access to the peak is via Laguna Lake.

Cheda Ranch
Stenner Creek Road
polyland.calpoly.edu/topics/recreation/x330/chedahike.htm
FREE!

From Highway 101 take the Santa Rosa Street/Highway 1 exit. Head north and continue straight out of town. Turn right onto Stenner Creek Road.

Park west of the trestle, then walk down the last paved road on the north before the trestle.

This relatively flat trail along Stenner Creek meanders past Middlecamp Reservoir, Nelson Reservoir and straight on to the Cheda Ranch milking barn with modern farm equipment viewable by the public. If the hike to the barn and back aren't enough, on the return trip to the car take the trail north around the east side of Nelson Reservoir. The trail climbs gently as it loops past Frog Pond to a view point overlooking the ranch, sheep unit and Chorro Valley.

Chorro Creek
Cal Poly Chorro Creek Road
polyland.calpoly.edu/topics/recreation/x330/chorrocanyon.htm
FREE!

From Highway 1, turn south onto Education Drive, then immediately right onto Cal Poly Chorro Creek Road

Although adjacent to the Cuesta College campus, this 582-acre ranchland is owned and maintained by Cal Poly. Take this generally flat, pleasant walk through vineyards, past a lagoon and down Chorro Creek. The path also leads past an "educational flying range" maintained by the university's College of Engineering and used regularly by local model aircraft enthusiasts.

C.L. Smith Joint Use Park

1375 Balboa Street adjacent to C.L. Smith Elementary School

(805) 781-7300

www.slocity.org/parksandrecreation

FREE!

From Highway 101 take Los Osos Valley Road west, turn right onto Oceanaire, then right onto Balboa Street.

This 4.8-acre park includes ball diamonds, athletic fields, play structures and basketball courts.

Cuesta Canyon County Park

East end of Loomis Street

(805) 781-5930

www.slocountyparks.org

☛ FREE!

From Highway 101 take the Grand Avenue exit. Take Grand Avenue north, and then turn right onto Loomis Street which feeds directly into the parking lot.

Although it appears to be in San Luis Obispo, Cuesta Park is a county park. San Luis Creek bubbles through the center of the park which also houses play structures, horseshoe pits, playing fields, picnic areas, large pit barbecues, a hiking trail and restrooms.

Dairy Creek Golf Course

El Chorro Regional Park, across Highway 1 from Cuesta College

(805) 782-8060

www.slocountyparks.com

$$-$$$

From Highway 101 take the Santa Rosa Street/Highway 1 exit and proceed north out of San Luis Obispo. About 5 miles past Highland Drive, turn right into El Chorro Regional Park and follow the signs to the course.

Reservations are accepted up to one week in advance for one of the newest public golf courses in San Luis Obispo County. The 18-hole, 6,548-yard, par 71 course designed by John Harbottle serves up some local challenges, not the least of which is the erratic coastal breeze that can whip across the fairways at a moment's notice. Fees are reduced for golfers under age 17, students and seniors. Cart rentals are available.

Dairy Creek is also home to the Central Coast Golf Academy. The training program offers short game seminars, equipment analysis, driving range, video analysis and stay-and-play golf for on-course strategy sessions.

Damon-Garcia Sports Fields
South Broad Street
(805) 781-7300
www.slocity.org/parksandrecreation
FREE!

From Highway 101 take the Los Osos Valley Road exit. Turn right onto Los Osos Valley Road, left onto South Higuera Street, right onto Tank Farm Road, then left onto Broad Street/Highway 227. The complex is on the left.

This 24-acre sports complex features a specialized grass designed to withstand the tests of turf sports. While there are no play structures at this new park as of press time, it remains a fine expanse of grass ideal for letting kids run out some of their bottled up energy.

East Cuesta Ridge
☞ FREE!

Take Highway 101 north out of San Luis Obispo and up Cuesta Grade (the big hill just north of town). Mt. Lowe Road is just past the summit on the right side of the road. The unsigned road is little more than an extended

pullout with room to park before the locked gate. (Note: The safest access is from northbound U.S. 101; access from southbound side absolutely not advised.)

Public access to this graded dirt road is limited to pedestrian and bicycle use. The winding road ascends 7 ½ miles to and along the ridge high above the highway and canyons and past two radio facilities, native oak groves and several peaks including Mt. Lowe, Black Butte, Lopez Mountain and Gay Mountain. The long, unrelenting climb can be grueling for small children and adults unaccustomed to such ascents, but the road provides clear and relatively smooth travel. The views from the top are among the best in the area, and the ride down is invigorating.

El Chorro Regional Park
Off Highway 1 about 5 miles north of Highland Drive
(805) 781-5930
www.slocountyparks.com

☞ FREE!

From Highway 101, take the Santa Rosa Street/Highway 1 exit and turn north and continue about 5 miles past the city limits.

This 490-acre county park has unique play structures, artificial rocks for bouldering, 62 campsites, three trails, a fenced dog park, barbecue facilities, volleyball courts, horseshoe pits, softball fields, an 18-hole golf course and a busy calendar of events. The park is also home to the 150-acre San Luis Obispo Botanical Garden (805-546-3501) and Education Center which provides exhibits about the garden and sustainable design such as straw bale construction and passive solar heating.

Hikes in the park include Dairy Creek (a 1.2-mile, stroller-friendly, relatively smooth, flat trail), Eagle Rock (a strenuous ¾-mile climb culminating in expansive views of the Chorro Valley) and the moderately strenuous, 1½-mile Oak Woodland Trail. Watch for poison oak, Chumash mortar holes, oak woodlands, wood rat nests, and plentiful native wildflowers including shooting stars, sticky monkey flower, popcorn flower, soap plant, wild rose and meadow lupine.

Ellsford Park
San Luis Drive between California Boulevard and Cazadero Street
(805) 781-7300
www.slocity.org/parksandrecreation
FREE!

From Highway 101, take the California Boulevard exit. Go south on California Boulevard, turn left onto San Luis Drive.

Two grassy areas compose this pocket park that totals 1 acre. The park features benches and an extremely steep drop off to creek.

Emerson Park
Bounded by Nipomo, Pacific, Pismo and Beach streets
(805) 781-7300
www.slocity.org/parksandrecreation
FREE!

From Highway 101 take the Marsh Street exit and continue straight into town. Turn right onto Nipomo Street.

This city-block park was once the home of Emerson School. Today the park includes a playing field installed by the parents of Emerson School students decades ago. More recent additions include play structures, adult fitness zone, community garden, basketball courts, picnic tables and the city's parks and recreation department headquarters.

French Park
Poinsettia Street
(805) 781-7300
www.slocity.org/parksandrecreation

FREE!

From Highway 101 take the Los Osos Valley Road exit. Turn right onto Los Osos Valley Road, left onto South Higuera Street, right onto Tank Farm Road, and then right onto Poinsettia Street.

This 10-acre park includes a multi-use court, youth baseball/softball field, sand volleyball court, tennis court, horseshoe pits, barbecue areas, picnic tables, play structures and a restroom.

Islay Hill Park
Tank Farm and Orcutt roads
(805) 781-7300
www.slocity.org/parksandrecreation
FREE!

From Highway 101 take the Los Osos Valley Road exit. Turn right onto Los Osos Valley Road, left onto South Higuera Street, and right onto Tank Farm Road.

This popular 5-acre neighborhood park features play structures, youth baseball/softball field, basketball court, tennis court, sand volleyball court and picnic areas.

Irish Hills Natural Reserve
access from Prefumo Canyon Road
(805) 781-7300
www.slocity.org/parksandrecreation
FREE!

Take Highway 101 to Los Osos Valley Road exit. Turn west onto Los Osos Valley Road, then turn left onto Prefumo Canyon Road. About one-tenth of a mile after leaving the last neighborhood, watch for a locked gate on the left side of the road. Park alongside the roadway.

Eventually city officials hope to create a trail system linking San Luis Obispo to Montana de Oro State Park to the west. When they do, the Irish Hills will be the jumping off point. Until then, the 340-acre reserve provides opportunities for pleasant family adventures on foot, mountain bike or horseback.

Within a 30-minute hike from the Prefumo Canyon Trailhead, sweeping views from the ridge encompass the entire chain of morros, or mountains. The hike along the main trail is moderate. Loose gravel and a continuous incline pose the greatest challenges. The trail is often rutted in spots, but there are no big surprises. Side trails take visitors to caves and views. Throughout much of the area, shade is in short supply. There are no watering holes or facilities along the way, so plan accordingly.

Trailside flora includes plenty of poison oak, monkey flower, white globe lily or white fairy lantern, Scotch broom, larkspur, and Indian paintbrush. Wildlife is often spotted here including deer, foxes, and a variety of reptiles and birds.

THE IRISH HILLS NATURAL PRESERVE provides ample hiking and cycling opportunities.

Islay Hill Open space
Tank Farm Road east of Broad Street
(805) 781-7300
www.slocity.org/parksandrecreation
FREE!

From Highway 101 take the Los Osos Valley Road exit. Turn right onto Los Osos Valley Road, left onto South Higuera Street, and right onto Tank Farm Road.

This local hike has grown more popular with the development of neighborhoods nearby and a conveniently placed public parking lot at the park near its base. The climb is strenuous, but short as the area's peaks go, and affords a great view. Beware of the poison oak along the trail and at the top.

Islay/French Parks Bike Path
(805) 781-7300
www.slocity.org/parksandrecreation
FREE!

From Highway 101 take the Los Osos Valley Road exit. Turn right onto Los Osos Valley Road, left onto South Higuera Street, and right onto Tank Farm Road.

This winding bike/pedestrian path invites trikes, strollers and scooters, too, on its course connecting two neighborhood parks. A set of stairs midway along the path adds a bit of a challenge.

Johnson Park

1020 Southwood Drive

(805) 781-7300

www.slocity.org/parksandrecreation

FREE!

From Highway 101 take the Los Osos Valley Road exit. Turn right onto Los Osos Valley Road, left onto South Higuera Street, and right onto Tank Farm Road. Turn left onto Broad Street / Highway 227, left onto Orcutt Road, then left onto Laurel Lane. Turn left onto Southwood Drive. The park is on the right between the YMCA and the eucalyptus trees.

This oft-shaded 4 1/2-acre park includes play structures, barbecue area, multi-use court, picnic tables, restrooms, outdoor basketball courts and a bike path along the creek.

Laguna Golf Course

11175 Los Osos Valley Road

(805) 781-7309

www.slocity.org/parksandrecreation/golf.asp

$

From Highway 101 take the Los Osos Valley Road exit and proceed north to the course on the left side of the road.

The city's parks department prides itself on offering affordable golf for the whole family on this 9-hole, 2,612-yard, par-60 executive course. The course, driving range, club, cart rentals and lessons are available from 7 a.m. to dusk daily.

Laguna Hills Park

Bounded by Valecito and San Adriano courts and Mirada Drive

(805) 781-7300

www.slocity.org/parksandrecreation

FREE!

From Highway 101 take Los Osos Valley Road west. Turn left onto Diablo Drive, and then left onto Mirada Drive.

This neighborhood park on 3½ acres includes a play area and picnic tables, but no restrooms.

Laguna Lake Natural Reserve

500 Madonna Road

(805) 781-7300

www.slocity.org/parksandrecreation

FREE!

From Highway 101 take the Madonna Road exit and turn west.

The city's 360-acre reserve features a system of hiking trails for varying abilities. Take a gentle walk along the flats or climb up Cerro San Luis. This park is immediately adjacent to Laguna Lake Park.

Laguna Lake Park

500 Madonna Road

(805) 781-7300

www.slocity.org/parksandrecreation

FREE!

From Highway 101 take the Madonna Road exit and turn west.

This 220-acre park has everything a city park needs and then some: play structures, dog park, hiking trails, barbecue areas, sand volleyball court, fitness trail and a 180-acre lake that can be used for fishing, sail boarding, row boating, and power boating under 1 horsepower. The park is adjacent to the city's 360-acre Laguna Lake Natural Reserve which features a system of hiking trails including access to Cerro San Luis.

LAGUNA LAKE NATURAL RESERVE

Las Praderas Park

Mariposa Drive

(805) 781-7300

www.slocity.org/parksandrecreation

FREE!

From Highway 101 turn east onto Los Osos Valley Road. Turn left onto South Higuera Street and left onto Praderas Drive. The park is at the T intersection of Praderas and Mariposa drives.

A pocket park of grass on nearly a quarter acre.

Leaning Pine Arboretum

Via Carta, Cal Poly

www.leaningpinearboretum.calpoly.edu

FREE!

From Highway 101, take the Grand Avenue exit north onto the Cal Poly campus, stopping for a parking pass at the information booth immediately upon entering campus. Continue along Grand Avenue, turn right onto

Perimeter Road, and turn right onto Via Carta. The plant shop and greenhouse are on the right directly across from the horse stables.

Families with well-supervised children are welcome to picnic or simply wander the 5-acre grounds of the arboretum from 10 a.m. to 5 p.m. Mondays through Saturdays when school is in sessions. Pick up a garden walk guide at the kiosk near the entrance or in the neighboring Cal Poly Plant Shop. Interpretive signs also offer a bit of education, or make a reservation for an interactive group tour.

Visitors are asked to stay on designated paths. Gardeners use reclaimed water throughout the garden, so children should be strongly discouraged from playing in any water, puddles, hoses, taps or other water sources within the garden.

The arboretum is also home to a variety of special events throughout the year.

Meadow Park
Meadow Avenue at South Street
(805) 781-7300
www.slocity.org/parksandrecreation
FREE!

From Highway 101, take the Madonna Road exit and head east. Turn left onto South Higuera Street, then immediately right onto South Street. Turn right onto Meadow Avenue.

This 14-acre park offers plenty of room to run, fly kites or throw a ball. The park includes barbecue areas, horseshoe pits, sand volleyball courts, basketball court, fitness course, walking trails, playground, softball field and restrooms.

Mission Plaza
Monterey Street between Chorro and Broad streets
☛ FREE!

From Highway 101 take the Marsh Street exit. Turn right onto Chorro Street. The mission is on the right midway through the second block.

This open-air walkway between Mission San Luis Obispo de Tolosa and San Luis Creek is a fun place to let the kids run, give parents a rest and take in any of a number of public events held throughout the year such as the I Madonnari Italian Street Painting Festival, Plein Air Festival and Concerts in the Plaza, a live music series held every Friday evening throughout summer months. Children delight in feeding ducks or tossing rocks in San Luis Creek below the bridge. A shallow fountain in front of the mission features Paula Zima's "Qiqsmu" sculpture depicting a Chumash girl, a bear and two cubs. There are benches and grassy mounds nearby for the weary. The plaza also includes public restrooms, an amphitheater, an arbor patio area, the historic Murray Adobe and access to San Luis Creek.

Mitchell Park

Bounded by Santa Rosa, Pismo, Buchon and Osos streets

(805) 781-7300

www.slocity.org/parksandrecreation

FREE!

From Highway 101 take Marsh Street and drive straight into downtown. Turn right onto Osos Street.

This city center park encompasses an entire city block. Amenities include play structures, a bandstand, horseshoe pit, picnic tables, a barbecue area and restrooms.

Osos/Triangle Park

Osos Street and Railroad Avenue

(805) 781-7300

www.slocity.org/parksandrecreation

FREE!

From Highway 101 take the Marsh Street exit and continue straight into town. Turn right onto Osos Street. The park is on the left at the Y intersection of Osos Street and Santa Barbara Street.

A one-third-acre grassy triangle of a pocket park with one picnic table.

Pennington Ranch

(805) 756-1111

polyland.calpoly.edu/topics/recreation/x330/pennington%20hike.htm

FREE!

From Highway 1 north of San Luis Obispo, turn right onto Education Way, turn right at the Y onto Pennington Creek Road, continue past the ranch, and over a bridge. The trailhead is past the first gate on the left after the bridge.

This relatively little-known Cal Poly property is open to hikers and mountain bikers. With few visitors, wildlife abounds here. Watch for deer, coyotes and bring binoculars for birding. The trailhead leads right onto the old sheep unit. Don't be alarmed, just carry on straight through to the trail on the far side.

The easiest portion of the trail leads along Pennington Creek to a grove of olive trees at the confluence of four creeks. Families with small children not used to hiking or inclines may want to turn back here.

For a more lengthy (and more challenging) hike, continue along the loop trail past the stone corral, around the north side and eventually the top of the hill, then follow a four-wheel-drive road along the ridge and back to the dirt road.

Poly Canyon

Poly Canyon Road, Cal Poly campus

(805) 756-1111

www.polyland.calpoly.edu

☞ FREE!

From Highway 101, take the Grand Avenue exit north onto the Cal Poly campus, stopping for a parking pass at the information booth immediately upon entering campus. Turn right onto Perimeter Road, then right onto Poly Canyon Road. An often-locked gate keeps out motorists, but bicycles, pedestrians and equestrians are welcome.

A graded dirt road along Brizzolara Creek gives way to a variety of hiking, biking and equestrian trails that meander to the Design Village, scenic ridges and eventually to Stenner Creek. All trails discussed in this section can be walked in either direction.

The most difficult thing about Poly Canyon is finding parking. For a quick and easy answer to legal parking, stop at the information booth at the Grand Avenue entrance to campus. Parking permits (required) are also sold there.

Once at the Poly Canyon gate (which is often locked since vehicular access beyond the gate is supposed to be limited to residents and campus authorities), enjoy an easy stroll on the well-maintained, graded dirt road.

There are several trail options.

About three-quarters of a mile from the gate are a trail and bridge on the right side of the road. Follow this sometimes steep climb through a swale and finally to the ridge above the Poly "P" east of the dorms. Once on the ridge, the walk is easy and often breezy. This loop can be completed by following the path down the western slope of the hill with a quick stop for an alphabet lesson atop the "P."

The most unusual stop in the canyon is Design Village, a 9-acre experimental architectural design and construction area in a park-like setting. To find the village, take the easy walk up Poly Canyon Road past the "P" fork. Take the trail that passes under the stone archway to the left of the road and follow the clearly marked pathway to the village. A handful of architecture students live in the canyon which is also home to the annual international Design Village competition started here in 1974. Existing structures particularly attractive to many children include the shell house, tensile structure, stick house, underground house, geodesic dome and the canyon's

Birding at Design Village in POLY CANYON

first student-built landmark: the 1963 concrete blade structure which was rebuilt in 2004.

For a longer, more challenging loop, continue along the main road about 25 yards past the stone archway to the gate on your left. Hop the gate and continue along this road as it turns to single track, loops around the backside of the knoll before heading back downhill through Horse Canyon and back to the main campus.

The Great Loop is a 6.5-mile trail that also can begin in Poly Canyon. Rather than turn left and climb the gate, continue straight on through the gates at Patterson Ranch, a Poly-owned property, being sure to leave all gates as you found them. This loop trail continues up the hill toward the train tracks, along

Studying nature inside POLY CANYON'S dome

the hillside, then back down Stenner Creek Canyon past working ranches, an impressive train trestle, the campus farms and back to the main campus.

Trails are numerous in the canyon. For detailed information, check the Cal Poly website or the biking and hiking books listed in the resources section of this book.

Prefumo Canyon Road
FREE!
Take Highway 101 to Los Osos Valley Road exit. Turn west onto Los Osos Valley Road, then turn left onto Prefumo Canyon Road.

This is a beautiful drive, walk or bike along a winding canyon road that meanders through oak groves and over San Luis Obispo's legendary rolling hills. Views from the 1,360-foot summit are spectacular during the day, but the area is equally popular at night for stargazers seeking dark skies away from any viewing obstacles.

Double back and return to San Luis Obispo or continue on to See Canyon and Avila Valley.

Priolo-Martin Park
Vista del Collados at Vista del Arroyo
(805) 781-7300
www.slocity.org/parksandrecreation

FREE!

From Highway 101 turn west onto Los Osos Valley Road. Turn right onto Descanso Street, then left onto Vista del Arroyo.

A quarter-acre pocket park with trail and benches featuring views across Laguna Lake to Cerro San Luis and Bishop Peak.

Railroad Recreational Trail

(805) 781-7300

www.slocity.org/parksandrecreation

FREE!

From Highway 101 take the Marsh Street exit and follow Marsh into town. Turn right onto Osos Street and continue straight. Follow the jog to the left at the triangular park, then park in the lot near the rail station.

This 1.2-mile trail from Orcutt Road to the Jennifer Street Bridge offers an alternative to street cycling for families. The route follows the southwest perimeter of Sinsheimer Park, a good place to stop for a rest, a picnic or a jaunt through the play structure.

Reservoir Canyon Natural Reserve

Reservoir Road about 1 mile north of San Luis Obispo off Highway 101

(805) 781-7300

www.slocity.org/parksandrecreation

☛ **FREE!**

Take Highway 101 north through San Luis Obispo. After the last SLO exit (Monterey Street), watch closely for side roads. The second right is Reservoir Canyon Road. Turn right here. Follow the road to the dirt parking area near the locked gate.

Ask locals about Reservoir Canyon and they're likely to shrug blankly, but the city has owned acreage in the canyon for more than a century. The long-abandoned reservoir and the old road leading to it returned to nature decades ago, but they left behind a clear path that offers a pleasant creekside hike through cool, dense shade of sycamore and oak minutes away from the city center.

The trail through the city's 520-acre open space meanders along Reservoir Creek, which can run briskly in winter storms then slow to a trickle by early autumn. The route is not stroller friendly and bicycles are not allowed. Smaller children who are relatively sure of foot will have no problem following the gurgling creek. Further along, parents may have to take over as a steady grade leads to fantastic canyon views. At any rate, watch for poison oak which is prevalent here.

The city plans to continue the trail west over the ridge to Johnson Avenue.

San Luis Blues
SLO Stadium, Sinsheimer Park
Southwood Drive
www.bluesbaseball.com
(805) 547-9929
$-$$$

From Highway 101 take the Los Osos Valley Road exit. Turn right onto Los Osos Valley Road, left onto South Higuera Street, and right onto Tank Farm Road. Turn left onto Broad Street/Highway 227, left onto Orcutt Road, then left onto Laurel Lane. Turn left onto Southwood Drive.

This summer collegiate baseball program provides a professional atmosphere and top amateur play Memorial Day weekend through early August. General admission is $7, but the $25 family pass for two adults and two children includes four admissions, four hot dogs, four sodas and a bag of nut. (Non-family groups of four get a similar deal for $30.)

San Luis Creek
Various points throughout San Luis Obispo
FREE!
San Luis Creek was the mission's first source of water. Today its route through the city is mostly under streets and buildings. The easternmost public access to San Luis Creek is at Reservoir Canyon. The creek serves as a popular stop for visitors to Cuesta County Park where it sometimes meanders, sometimes rushes through the park before heading into a residential neighborhood and, finally, into the tunnels. The creek sees daylight again at Mission Plaza where it is a popular spot for ducks, families and downtown business people. Here it includes two blocks of walkways, parks, benches, viewing areas, bridges and boulder crossings within view of creekside shops and restaurants.

Santa Rosa Park
Santa Rosa and Oak streets
(805) 781-7300
www.slocity.org/parksandrecreation
FREE!
From Highway 101, take Santa Rosa Street/Highway 1 north.

The 11-acre park includes play structures, barbecue areas, horseshoe pits, softball field, baseball field, basketball/roller hockey court, restrooms and San Luis Obispo Skate Park.

Sinsheimer Park

North end of Southwood Drive

(805) 781-7300

www.slocity.org/parksandrecreation

FREE!

From Highway 101 take the Los Osos Valley Road exit. Turn right onto Los Osos Valley Road, left onto South Higuera Street, and right onto Tank Farm Road. Turn left onto Broad Street/Highway 227, left onto Orcutt Road, then left onto Laurel Lane. Turn left onto Southwood Drive. The park is at the end of the drive.

This 23½-acre sports complex is home to San Luis Obispo Baseball Stadium, Stockton Softball Field and the SLO Swim Center which features an Olympic-sized outdoor heated pool, tot pool, locker rooms and restrooms. The park also includes batting cages, tennis courts, play structure, sand volleyball court, running and bike trails, horseshoe pit and barbecue areas. The pool is open daily for lap swim and has regularly scheduled recreation swim hours. It is also home to the San Luis Obispo Swim Club and serves as the home pool for San Luis Obispo High School swimming, diving and water polo.

South Hills Open space

(805) 781-7300

www.slocity.org/parksandrecreation

FREE!

There are two main accesses. For the northwestern access, from Highway 101 take the Madonna Road exit from Highway 101. Turn right onto Madonna Road, left onto South Higuera then immediately right onto South Street. Turn right onto Exposition. For the southeastern access, continue along South Street, turn right onto Broad Street, right onto Stoneridge Drive and left onto Bluerock Drive. The trailhead is at the back of Stoneridge Park on the right.

This 90-acre preserve includes a prominent ridge that divides the southern portion of the city. Trails are open to pedestrian traffic only. From the pocket park off Bluerock Drive, the trail offers an easy walk up an abandoned road to the ridge where views of the city and nearby peaks are superb. The top of the ridge is a great place to teach kids about the state rock, serpentinite, which abounds here.

Red Fox,
SOUTH HILLS OPEN
SPACE

SOUTH HILLS OPEN SPACE provides unexpected views, relatively easy hikes and a quick getaway only a few minutes walk from downtown. Like some of the city's other open space preserves, South Hills trails are not open for mountain bikers. Those who slow down long enough for a hike here are rewarded with cool afternoon breezes, spectacular views, wildflower displays and the occasional visit from area wildlife.

Stagecoach Road
Somewhat parallel to U.S. 101 north of San Luis Obispo to
Cuesta Ridge
FREE!

*To begin at the top, take Highway 101 north out of San Luis Obispo and up
Cuesta Grade (the big hill just north of town). A left-hand-turn lane at
Cuesta Summit leads the way to the old road. Once off the freeway, take a left
onto Stagecoach Road. The graded dirt road meanders down the canyon wall
and back to Highway 101. To begin at the bottom, take Highway 101 north to
Stagecoach Road, (the first handy left past Monterey Street).*

The old dirt road that once served as the main route for the stage line
remains open as a public thoroughfare. The unrelenting incline winds
through oak groves to the summit goal. It is a fun ride for fit cyclists
interested in out-and-back rides as well as skilled riders interested in a
somewhat technical and potentially speedy descent that drops down the Cal
Poly side of the mountain.

Stenner Springs Open Space
End of Stenner Canyon Road
(805) 781-7300
www.slocity.org/parksandrecreation
FREE!

*From Highway 101 take the Santa Rosa Street/Highway 1 exit. Head north
and continue straight out of town. Turn right onto Stenner Creek Road which
ends at the open space.*

Forty-nine acres with limited hiking trails that are minimally maintained.

Stoneridge Park
Bluerock Drive
(805) 781-7300
www.slocity.org/parksandrecreation
FREE!

*From Highway 101 take the Madonna Road exit from Highway 101. Turn
right onto Madonna Road, left onto South Higuera then immediately right
onto South Street, right onto Broad Street, right onto Stoneridge Drive and
left onto Bluerock Drive.*

A half-acre grassy pocket park with picnic tables and trailhead for the
South Hills Open Space hiking trails.

Terrace Hill
(805) 781-7300
www.slocity.org/parksandrecreation
FREE!

*From Highway 101 take California Boulevard south, turn right onto San
Luis Drive, left onto Johnson Avenue, and then right onto Bishop Street.*

Though one in the same series of volcanic peaks that dominate the city's skyline, Terrace Hill is but a large mound begging to be hiked. With a peak of just 501 feet and a passable trail, this is a good place to let the kids take a run up (and down, and up, and down) the hill, a longtime favorite with local athletic teams and keen individuals.

Throop Park
510 Cerro Romauldo Ave
(805) 781-7300
www.slocity.org/parksandrecreation
FREE!
From Highway 101 turn north onto Highway 1, left onto Foothill Boulevard, right onto Ferrini Road and left onto Cerro Romauldo Avenue.
This neighborhood park includes play structure, picnic tables and restroom.

Vista Lago Park
Vista del Lago at Laguna Lane
(805) 781-7300
www.slocity.org/parksandrecreation
FREE!
From Highway 101 take Los Osos Valley Road west, turn right onto Laguna Lane, then right onto Vista del Lago.
A ½-acre pocket park with picnic and play areas.

West Cuesta Ridge
FREE!
Take Highway 101 north out of San Luis Obispo and up Cuesta Grade (the big hill just north of town). A left-hand-turn lane at Cuesta Summit leads the way to TV Tower Road that generally follows the ridge. Once off the freeway, take a right and continue up the poorly maintained road (and watch for nasty potholes among other obstacles).
The highlight of this ridge is the view west along the morros to the Pacific Ocean. A 1,334-acre botanical area featuring Sargent cypress trees is also worth a stop on this national forest land. The trees occur naturally only in California. The dirt road that extends from Highway 101 is popular among mountain bikers and motorists seeking out scenic views. The ridge and associated trails are great places to see spring wildflowers and to sneak above the marine layer for sunrise or sunset. The ridge trail from the botanical area to Cerro Alto is a popular route among fit area hikers and mountain bikers.

The dirt road can be terribly rough for passenger cars, particularly those with low clearance. This road is not recommended for vehicles with trailers or RVs due to tight turns, potholes and other obstacles along the route.

YMCA
1020 Southwood Drive
(805) 543-8235
www.sloymca.org
FREE!-$$$

From Highway 101 take the Los Osos Valley Road exit. Turn right onto Los Osos Valley Road, left onto South Higuera Street, and right onto Tank Farm Road. At Broad Street/Highway 227 turn left, turn right onto Orcutt Road, turn left onto Laurel Lane, and then turn left onto Southwood Drive.

This American standby offers after school programs, family fun nights, racquetball courts, more than 40 class offerings, fun runs, special events, specialty camps, and fitness memberships that include access to Sinsheimer Pool. Kids Gym, a preschool program held in two-hour sessions from 8:30 a.m. to 2:30 p.m., includes activities for $5 per child per session. Children must be potty trained. Healthy Kids Club is a drop-in program for older children held daily from 2:30 p.m. to 7 p.m. There are also occasional free events including Halloween at the YMCA and Happy Holidays at the YMCA. Call for current offerings.

OTHER ADVENTURES

Apple Farm Inn Millhouse
2015 Monterey St.
(805) 544-2040
www.applefarm.com
FREE!

From northbound Highway 101 take the Monterey Street exit. Continue straight onto Monterey Street for about half a block. From southbound Highway 101, take the Monterey Street exit, turn left at the top of the ramp, then left onto Monterey Street.

The replica of a 19th Century millhouse at this inn and restaurant is probably the most interesting part of the property to children (and many adults). Bring the kids to watch the miller make ice cream, press cider or perform other feats with machinery that utilizes the 14-foot working waterwheel. The mill generally works weekends, but call in advance to check current schedule.

The property also includes a hotel and a restaurant featuring desserts large enough for a small family to share (not that you'll want to).

Automobilia Museum at McCarthy's Wholesale
11 Higuera St.
(805) 544-1900
www.mccarthywholesale.com/?content=210
FREE!

From Highway 101 take the Madonna Road exit and head east, then turn right onto Higuera Street.

Although this property is primarily a used-car lot, the showroom includes a collection of antique and specialty cars, glass cases full of toy cars and other automotive and air travel goodies.

Bubblegum Alley
700 block of Higuera Street
☞ FREE!

From Highway 101 take the Marsh Street exit. Follow Marsh into town, turn left onto Garden Street then left onto Higuera Street. The pedestrian-only alley is on the left side of the street midway between Garden and Broad streets.

In a town surrounded by beautiful mountains, filled with parks and packed with activities ideal for families, it may seem odd to point out a spot where people have been spitting out their gum for nearly half a century. Some call the alley lined with discarded chewed gum absolutely disgusting; others call it a hoot. Kids usually just ask for a piece of gum to chew so they can make their marks on the wall.

No one knows exactly when the gum collection began, but local lore has it that some time in the 1950s kids started slapping their gum on the wall. It may have been a team tradition, or merely a place to put their gum. Some gum artists have opted to make more extravagant marks. Some have

Watch those little fingers in BUBBLEGUM ALLEY where some artifacts are decades old.

chewed stick upon stick of gum in a concerted effort to spell complete words, leave their Greek letters or sculpt more detailed contributions.

Love it or hate it, Bubblegum Alley serves as a point of interest in which children delight.

Cal Poly Associated Students Inc. Epicenter

Second floor, Julian McPhee University Union

(805) 756-1281

www.asi.calpoly.edu

FREE!

From Highway 101, take the Grand Avenue exit north onto the Cal Poly campus, stopping for a parking pass at the information booth immediately upon entering campus. Continue north on Grand Avenue to Perimeter Road.

One-stop shopping for student-sponsored activities, many of which are open to the general public.

Cal Poly Athletics

(866) 756-7267 (tickets)

(805) 756-2924

www.gopoly.com

FREE!-$$$

This university offers all sorts of athletic programs for its students, which means plenty of opportunities for fans. Catch a ball game, swim meet, tennis match or other sporting event with the family.

Cal Poly Associated Students Inc. Children's Center

Building 133 on Campus Way

(805) 756-1267

www.calpoly.edu

$$$

From Highway 101, take the California Boulevard exit and head north. Turn right onto Campus Way.

The center provides daycare for children ages 4 months to 6 years. It also runs Poly Trekkers, a summer program for school-age children.

Crux Climbing Gym

1160 Laurel Lane

(805) 544-2789

www.cruxslo.com

$$

From Highway 101 take the Los Osos Valley Road exit. Turn right onto Los Osos Valley Road, left onto South Higuera Street, and right onto Tank Farm Road. Turn left onto Broad Street/Highway 227, left onto Orcutt Road, then left onto Laurel Lane. The gym is on the left.

This indoor climbing facility offers bouldering, lead climbing with auto-belay systems, ropes, rope ladders and a rest area where visitors can play board games, watch climbing videos or read on comfy mats and couches. One-time training is required and there is a $10 per person training fee. Full-day admission for climbers younger than 14 is $10. Adult admission is $12. Minimum age is 4, but staff leaves it to parents' discretion for little avid climbers. Call for hours, which vary by season and include hours set aside specifically for youth and family climbers.

Cuesta College
Highway 1
(805) 546-3100
www.cuesta.edu
FREE!-$$
From Highway 101, take the Santa Rosa Street/Highway 1 exit and turn north. Continue out of town about 5 miles to the college.

Cuesta Community College is home to galleries, theatrical and musical performances. For current listings, check academic.cuesta.edu/finearts/events_info.htm. The college also welcomes the public to athletic events. For schedules, check academic.cuesta.edu/athletics.

The campus also includes a beautiful outdoor swimming pool complex open for student and public programs (www.communityprograms.net). The complex includes an Olympic-sized pool with the area's only 3-meter diving board. Seasonal aquatic offerings for youth have included water polo camp, swimming lessons and diving classes. For pool information, call (805) 546-3207.

Downtown Trolley
Serving downtown – hours vary
(805) 781-2777
www.rideshare.org/buses/slotransit.htm
$
Pickup points along Monterey Street: in front of the Apple Farm Restaurant, Grand Avenue, California Boulevard, Toro Street, across the street from Fremont Theater, and ½ block east of Mission Plaza. Other pickup points include Higuera Street between Chorro and Garden Streets, Nipomo Street just outside Foster's Freeze, Marsh Street at Chorro Street and Osos Street ½-block south of Monterey Street.

Small children delight in every form of transportation. For an inexpensive thrill, hop on the trolley that connects downtown with the hotels on the north end of Higuera Street. Ride a block or take the whole loop.

Hours vary. Children ride free; adults ride for 50 cents. The Downtown Trolley runs Thursdays from 3:30 p.m. to 9 p.m. (on modified route due to Thursday Night Farmers' Market), Fridays and Saturdays from noon to 9 p.m. and on Sundays from 10 a.m. to 3:30 p.m.

Islay Hill Alpaca Ranch

1165 Farmhouse Lane

(805) 545-8757

www.islayhillalpacas.com

FREE!

From Highway 101 take the Los Osos Valley Road exit. Turn right onto Los Osos Valley Road, left onto South Higuera Street, and right onto Tank Farm Road. Turn right onto Broad Street/Highway 227, then left onto Farmhouse Lane.

Call for a tour of this facility that raises alpaca for wool. Alpaca-related products including clothing and yarn are also sold here. Open by request.

KSBY

1772 Calle Joaquin

(805) 541-6666

www.ksby.com

FREE!

From Highway 101 head west onto Los Osos Valley Road. Take an immediate left onto Calle Joaquin and follow the road to the top of the hill.

This local television station offers public group tours by appointment only. The tour has traditionally given visitors an in-depth look at how television shows are made, with special emphasis on news broadcasting.

Madonna Inn

100 Madonna Road

(805) 543-3000

www.madonnainn.com

FREE!-$$$

From Highway 101 take the Madonna Road exit and turn west. Madonna Inn is on the right.

For half a century the family of Alex and Phyllis Madonna has owned and operated its original inn featuring 109 uniquely decorated rooms, many of which include features such as rock or waterfall showers. Take a tour for a look at the Cave Room, Yosemite Rock Room or even the Yahoo Room which features a bed on a buckboard.

Enjoy a tea and pastry party in the Copper Café, or check out the swinging lady and other features decorating the inn's various dining areas. Young men may be particularly interested in using the restrooms (and the girls can peek in once the coast is clear). No white porcelain for this family of creative minds. Instead, Alex Madonna installed a motion-activated waterfall urinal in the facility near the wine cellar. Another main restroom features a copper trough urinal complete with motion-activated waterwheel.

San Luis Obispo Children's Museum
1010 Nipomo Street
(805) 545-5874
www.slokids.org
☛ $

From Highway 101 take the Marsh Street exit and follow Marsh into town. Turn left onto Nipomo. The museum is two blocks up and on the right.

This three-story-tall children's museum has a history of providing great educational entertainment to children in a safe, friendly environment that is comfortable for kids and parents alike. Exhibits sponsored by local businesses, organizations and public service agencies provide hands-on fun. Interactive staff regularly schedules activiites, and the museum maintains a calendar of special events.

San Luis Obispo County Regional Airport
903 Airport Drive
(805) 781-5205
www.sloairport.com
FREE!

From Highway 101 take the Marsh Street exit and proceed straight into downtown, then turn left onto Broad Street. Continue out of town and then turn right on Airport Drive.

Still a relatively small town airport, this strip provides plenty of viewing area for young aeronautics enthusiasts.

Stenner Creek Trestle
Stenner Creek Road
FREE!

From Highway 101 take the Santa Rosa Street/Highway 1 exit. Head north and continue straight out of town. Turn right onto Stenner Creek Road.

This 953-foot-long, 90-foot-tall trestle was built on the East Coast, then shipped around Cape Horn for installation here in 1894. More than 100 years later it remains a signature portion of California's coastal rail route, and a nifty place to catch a different perspective of passing trains.

Sunset Drive-In Theater
255 Elks Lane
(805) 544-4475
www.rodkey.net/sunset_drivein.htm
☛ $

From northbound Highway 101 take the Prado Road exit and turn left onto Prado Road at the end of the offramp. From southbound Highway 101, take the Madonna Road exit, turn left onto Madonna Road, right onto Higuera Street, then left onto Prado Road at the old cemetery.

For a fun, affordable, all-American family night gather pillows, beanbags, sleeping bags, beach chairs, mattresses (whatever makes you comfortable) and head to one of only two drive-in theaters on the Central Coast. (The other is the Hi-Way Drive-In in Santa Maria.) The price is right for affordable family fun. If the movie is appropriate for youngsters, this might be just the place to introduce them to moving pictures on a big screen; children 5 and under get in free.

In the 1950s, these outdoor theaters were all the rage. Through the decades they dwindled, thousands closed, but San Luis Obispo never went without, and generations of families have enjoyed the experience together.

The best way to enjoy the drive-in is NOT in your own designated seats, but snuggled together in some fashion: a mattress in the bed of a pickup truck; comfy bean bags on the ground (or in aforementioned pickup); crammed in the back of the minivan, seats removed, hatch up; side by side in beach chairs; all while bundled under blankets as needed.

Thursday Night Farmers' Market

Higuera Street from Nipomo Street to Osos Street

(805) 781-2777

www.downtownslo.com/farmers.html

☛ FREE!

From Highway 101 take the Marsh Street exit and follow Marsh into town. Head straight for the Chorro Street parking structure on the right immediately past the intersection of Chorro and Marsh streets.

There are farmers' markets, then there's Thursday Night Farmers' Market in downtown San Luis Obispo. It's as much a street carnival as it is a market of fresh fruits, vegetables and flowers. Every week the street is closed to motorists for four hours to make room for thousands of pedestrians who spill from sidewalks to street to sample farmers' offerings, eat at various barbecues and enjoy live entertainment that ranges from bands to jugglers to belly dancers. There's always something of particular interest to children.

Setup begins at 5:30 p.m. every Thursday (only rain cancels), but vendors are strictly forbidden from selling before the 6 p.m. bell rings.

Chapter 2

Avila Beach & Port San Luis

The best sunbathing and swimming beach in San Luis Obispo County shares sheltered San Luis Bay with Port San Luis, Fishermen's Beach, Pirate's Cove and Olde Port Beach, also known among locals as Cal Poly Beach. Gentle waves lap the shore along this compact section of California coastline, providing fantastic opportunities for kayakers, paddlers, sailors, skim boarders, beginning surfers and body boarders.

Even when fog blankets the coast along the 160-mile stretch from Point Piños to Point Concepción, the sun pokes through at Avila Beach. While Pismo Beach, Oceano Dunes and the Guadalupe-Nipomo Dunes Complex bear the brunt of on-shore winds, Avila Beach enjoys protection from a jut of land that curves around the western edge of the bay.

Avila Valley, which stretches from Highway 101 to the beach, also serves up some interesting weather and family fun.

FISHERMEN'S BEACH offers great tidepooling when the tide is right. The Port San Luis Harbor District also includes Port San Luis Pier (background) and Avila Beach (not shown).

Presence of humans in the Avila area dates back some 5,000 years, according to the Port San Luis Harbor District, which serves these neighboring beaches. The area's modern history dates back to 1869 with the construction of People's Wharf. The town of Avila was founded five years later.

HISTORY

San Luis Obispo Light Station (aka Port Harford Lighthouse)
Pecho Coast Trail
(805) 541-8735
FREE!

From Highway 101 take Avila Beach Drive west through Avila Beach and park either in the Olde Port lot or in the pullout across the road from the power plant entrance.

Access is limited to docent-led hikes because the light station rests inside the current Diablo Canyon Nuclear Power Plant security buffer zone. Hikers who register at least 48 hours in advance for one of the semi-weekly hikes are rewarded with a beautiful adventure culminating in a tour around the light station property. The bluff top parcel includes the foghorn building and a duplex that once housed lighthouse keepers and their families. The light station is listed on the National Register of Historic Places.

Two routes are offered including the 3.5-mile round trip to the lighthouse and the 7.5-mile out-and-back to Rattlesnake Canyon, also with a stop at the lighthouse. Children over the age of 12 are welcome to join their adult hiking partners for this moderately strenuous round-trip hike along the edge of the Pacific. The age limit is strictly enforced.

NATURE

Avila Beach
(805) 595-5400
www.portsanluis.com
☛ FREE!

From Highway 101 take Avila Beach Drive west.

The best local beach for small children is Avila Beach with its gently sloping sand that encourages waders and young body boarders to venture into the sea. While lifeguards are on duty during summer months, parents should keep an eye on their little ones and weak swimmers should steer clear of waves, though they're typically small here during summer months.

Fishing is a popular activity from atop the pier where no fishing license is required. Other popular attractions include the old-fashioned, high-flying playground on the sand just west of the pier and the pirate-themed park just inland from the western end of the beach. The beach area also includes barbecues, picnic tables, restrooms, outdoor showers and the tile spiral of history inlaid in the pedestrian plaza east of the pier.

Bob Jones Trail
Ontario Road to Avila Beach Drive
☛ FREE!

From Highway 101 take San Luis Bay Drive west, then turn immediately left onto Ontario Road. The parking/staging area is on the left.

This 2½-mile paved pathway dedicated for walkers, bikers and skaters offers an easy, peaceful, scenic route through Avila Valley. Because it is largely flat and away from traffic, it is popular for families with young cyclists as well as strollers.

The path's inland terminus is off Ontario Road about one-third of a mile from San Luis Bay Drive. From there it winds along the route determined largely by San Luis Creek which it parallels. The path sneaks behind the orchards of Avila Valley Barn, the backside of the Sycamore Springs Resort Labyrinth and Mediation Garden before crossing San Luis Bay Drive. It later merges with the course pathways at Avila Beach Golf Resort before crossing heavily traveled Avila Beach Drive.

To lengthen your ride or walk, turn right onto Avila Beach Drive and continue to the road's end at Port San Luis. (Due to potentially heavy traffic, this portion is not recommended for young children or inexperienced riders/skaters.)

Fishermen's Beach
(805) 595-5400
www.portsanluis.com
FREE!

From Highway 101 take Avila Beach Drive west through Avila Beach, over the high bridge along the coast at San Luis Creek and past Olde Port Beach.

If Olde Port Beach wasn't small enough for you, try out Fishermen's Beach, as the westernmost stretch of sand is called. This little-advertised nook on the harbor is particularly nice for families more interested in digging in the sand and watching sailboats than surfing or playing on playgrounds.

It is only accessible at low tide.

Fishermen's Memorial
Eastern end of Port San Luis parking lot
(805) 595-5400
www.portsanluis.com
FREE!

From Highway 101 take Avila Beach Drive west through Avila Beach. The memorial is on the right side of the road shortly before the Olde Port parking lot at the end of Avila Beach Road.

A scenic spot for a picnic a short hop away from the sand. The dolphin fountain holds the interest of some kids long enough for them to enjoy their lunches at nearby picnic tables before returning to the sand or the car.

Pirate's Cove
Cave Landing Road
FREE!

From Highway 101 take Avila Beach Drive west. Turn left up the hill at Cave Landing Road which leads directly to a large, dirt parking area.

Whether or not a nude beach should be included in a family-oriented book may be a bone of contention, but the beauty of this cove is beyond reproach. If you're not afraid to take off your skivvies in public, or prefer to do so, venture half a mile up Cave Landing Road to Pirate's Cove. The picturesque cove is well protected from the wind by steep cliffs on three sides. The waves are ideal for frolicking but generally too small and shallow for good surfing.

Nudists strip down on the sand, but there are other aspects of this area that can be explored even by the most reserved, including a tunnel along the bluff from which fishing is quite popular.

Beach access is difficult due to a steep, unimproved trail down to the beach.

Olde Port Beach (aka Cal Poly Beach)
(805) 595-5400
www.portsanluis.com
FREE!

From Highway 101 take Avila Beach Drive west through Avila Beach and over the high bridge along the coast at San Luis Creek. Olde Port Beach is around the bend.

This lesser-known little stretch of sand nearly disappears at very high tides, but it is a great swimming beach with little or no wave action. Don't expect to catch the Last Great Wave here, but do bring along some hotdogs and firewood for an evening blaze. Fires are permitted in the heavy steel fire rings provided. (No pallet fires are allowed.) A vehicle ramp provides drive-on short-term access to the beach for dropping off/picking up supplies and loading/unloading watercraft. Dogs also run without leash on this rare stretch of canine-friendly sand.

Port San Luis Pier

(805) 595-5400

www.portsanluis.com

☛ FREE!

From Highway 101 take Avila Beach Drive west to its end.

Examining live fish at PORT SAN LUIS PIER

The Port San Luis pier draws fishermen venturing out for the hunt as well as landlubbers seeking to simply purchase fresh fish and crab. It remains a popular spot for pier fishing, commercial sport fishing, you-pick-'em live crab, a live seafood market and on-pier dining featuring fresh local fare. Patriot Sportfishing (805-595-7200) has long provided charter sportfishing cruises and offers whale watching tours generally from December to April.

Port San Luis Marine Institute

50 San Juan Street

(805) 595-7280

www.pslmi.org

$$$

From Highway 101 take Avila Beach Drive west to its end.

With a new museum/aquarium/community center in the works, this nonprofit educational facility may become more affordable. Meanwhile, its volunteers provide hands-on marine science education programs.

See Canyon

See Canyon Road between San Luis Bay Drive and Prefumo Canyon Road

FREE!

From Highway 101, take San Luis Bay Drive exit and
right onto See Canyon Road and follow the road to its p(
Prefumo Canyon Road then returns to San Luis Obispo (
Road.

This winding coastal canyon is home to apple orchards t
cooler conditions found here. Nights come earlier in this de
temperatures drop below that of other areas in the region c.   ...al
conditions for crisp apples. Longtime orchard standouts incl...ue:

Gopher Glen, 2899 See Canyon Road, (805) 595-2646,
www.gopherglen.com – More than 60 varieties of popular and heirloom
apples, kitchen shop, cookbooks, apple pears, fresh homemade cider, baskets
and fruit; open late July through October.

See Canyon Fruit Ranch, 2345 See Canyon Road, (805) 595-2775 -
focuses on old-time apple varieties; open September through October.

Sycamore Mineral Springs Labyrinth & Meditation Garden
1218 Avila Beach Drive
(805) 595-7302
www.smsr.com/labyrinth.html
☞ FREE!

From Highway 101 take Avila Beach Drive west.

It's fun to watch the kids' faces twist in confusion as they wind their way
first toward, then away from the center of the labyrinth before reaching

like a maze, there is only one path through the labyrinth, so way to get lost.

e adults may prefer a soothing massage at Sycamore Mineral Springs sort across the road, children seem more elated by some time in the tire swings and garden sunshine. The labyrinth and garden are owned by the resort which provides them both free to the public.

OTHER ADVENTURES

Avila Beach Golf Resort

6464 Ana Bay Drive

(805) 595-4000 ext. 1

www.avilabeachresort.com

$$-$$$

From Highway 101 take Avila Beach Drive west through Avila Beach, over the high bridge, and then take the first right.

This scenic golf resort welcomes young and experienced golfers alike. The par-71, 6,500-yard championship course runs from the oak-lined Avila Valley to the estuary just off Avila Beach. The resort offers clinics, lessons, a pro shop and restaurant.

Avila Valley Barn

560 Avila Beach Drive

(805) 595-2810

www.avilavalleybarn.com

☛ FREE!

From Highway 101 take Avila Beach Drive west. The barn is on the right just past Ontario Road.

What started as a simple roadside produce stand selling out of fruit crates quickly turned into one of the county's premier harvest season family attractions. Throughout summer and fall, the barn comes to life with a variety of produce from local growers and special events. Families are encouraged to pack their own lunches and enjoy picnics on the lawn under dancing trees, enjoy a day on the farm, feed and pet farm animals (just stop by the barn and ask for feed – staff gives away bags of scraps like corn husks and apple pieces), and pick produce from peaches to pumpkins.

The addition of a sweets shop featuring homemade ice cream complements the barn's collection of fresh-baked goods that have traditionally included breads, cakes, pies, turnovers and tarts.

Picking opportunities vary by season but generally follow this schedule: Olallieberries in May-June; peaches in July-August; apples in September-October; pumpkin picking and hay bale mazes each October; Christmas trees for sale (though not grown on site) in November. The barn generally closes in December and reopens in spring.

Avila Valley Hot Springs

250 Avila Beach Drive

(805) 595-2359

www.avilahotsprings.com

FREE!

From Highway 101 take Avila Beach Drive west.

Generations of families have enjoyed the naturally warm water of Avila Hot Springs. Visitors now enjoy a 50-foot-by-100-foot pool featuring 86-degree water, water slides and a 20-foot-by-20-foot mineral pool maintained at 104 degrees all year round.

Other facilities include a pizza kitchen, arcade, massage, barbecue and picnic areas, cabins and campgrounds boasting hot showers. The staff provides swimming lessons and summer swim camps. Generally open seven days a week from 8 a.m. to 8 p.m.

Diablo Canyon Nuclear Power Plant Public Information Center

6588 Ontario Road

9 a.m. to 1 p.m. Monday through Friday

(805) 546-5280

www.pge.com/education_training/about_energy/diablo_canyon/plant_tours/

FREE!

From Highway 101, take the San Luis Bay Drive exit and head west. Turn immediately left onto Ontario Road.

Self-guided exhibits provide information about the nearby nuclear power plant that generates up to 2,200 megawatts of electricity. Docents may be available to lead tours of the center by reservation.

The ROCK CAIRN near the labyrinth at Sycamore Mineral Springs Resort offers a hands-on lesson for inquisitive young artisans. The resort welcomes visitors to gently use the meditation garden where the cairns rests not far from tire swings, benches, the labyrinth and a scent garden.

Although SHELL BEACH is technically within Pismo Beach city limits, the area has a flavor all its own. While Pismo Beach is known for its vast expanse of sand and surf, Shell Beach is better known for its bluffs and tidepooling beaches. Surfers flock here when Pismo Beach is too crowded or too rough.

Chapter 3

Shell Beach

North of the ever-popular Pismo Beach and south of Avila Beach stretches a coastline full of cozy coves, bluff-top parks and public walkways. They're not exactly secret, but when Pismo Beach is crawling with visitors, Shell Beach coves remain relatively serene.

Technically part of the city of Pismo Beach, Shell Beach has long maintained its own identity. The relatively quiet neighborhood is bounded on one side by the Pacific Ocean and the other by Highway 101 and features spectacular ocean views.

Throughout its early years of construction, developers repeatedly found signs of Chumash history here: bones, household items, beads. Though the Chumash people and earliest investors saw the value of this spot, investors were slow to catch on. While the city near the pier was growing, Shell Beach remained a quiet farming area literally a stone's throw from the ocean.

After World War II the entire Central Coast saw a boom in real estate. Scenic Shell Beach was no exception.

Unlike its sandy southern portion, the attraction in this half of the city is in its coves where tide pooling, kayaking, beachcombing and sunbathing are popular activities. Although quiet coves beckon visitors at low tide, high tide often inundates the coves and, in some cases, brings waves crashing directly against the bluffs.

Swimming is permitted in all areas, and surfing is popular in many of them. Currents can be dangerous at all tides. There are no lifeguards on duty in any of the coves.

Kayaking is popular, offering visitors opportunities to get up close and personal with wildlife that forages in the kelp beds immediately offshore. Seals are plentiful, and dolphins are often spotted in the area. Local kayak rental and guide companies typically do not rent boats if conditions are too rough for boaters' safety, but parents should make their own assessment before taking children out.

The community is home to a plethora of parks from bluff perches to inland historical venues. All parks in Shell Beach are free and open during daylight hours. Many include picnic/barbecue areas and some have large group areas available by reservation.

NATURE

Bluffs Coastal Trail
Parking off Bluff Drive past the end of Indio Drive
(805) 773-7039
FREE!

From Highway 101 take Avila Beach Drive exit. Turn north onto Palisades Road, turn left onto El Portal Street, and then curve right onto Indio Drive, also known as Cave Landing Road. Drive around the median divider at the gated end of the road, and then turn right into a clearly marked parking lot built specifically for bluff trail traffic.

The easiest, most stroller-friendly walk in Shell Beach is also among the most scenic – a public walkway that winds along the bluff top at the far northern edge of Shell Beach in front of multi-million-dollar homes. The walk along paved trails is extremely easy and wheelchair accessible.

The 1-mile out-and-back paved pathway offers spectacular views south beyond the sandy expanse of Pismo Beach, over the Oceano State Vehicular Recreation Area and Guadalupe-Nipomo Dunes Complex and on toward Point Sal some 19 miles directly south. The view north includes Mallagh Landing (aka Pirate's Cove) and Point San Luis.

This trail is a great spot for introducing children to nature's scent garden, particularly in the spring when native plants are at their blooming peak. Hummingbirds swoop past visitors as they follow the trail to the Y that takes visitors down to the cove overlook. Though Pirate's Cove is a nude beach, the overlook was placed strategically to protect the privacy of sunbathers while providing a view of the beautiful cove. The viewpoint is ideal for spotting otters and seals.

A post fence keeps walkers on the paved trail most of the way, but at the overlook, a wide gap has been left in the fence, presumably so hikers may

BLUFFS COASTAL TRAIL in Shell Beach is among the most stroller friendly in the area.

continue, at their own risk, closer toward the edge. The portion of trail beyond the asphalt path is very rough, not maintained and dangerous. The area beyond the fence is **not** safe.

Though the pathway is intended for pedestrians, a fun paved, loop bike ride for experienced cyclists begins and ends at the pathway parking lot. Follow Cave Landing Road north past the big homes, up and down the bluff-top hills, past the cove parking lot and down the backside to Avila Beach Drive. Turn right onto Avila Beach Drive and pedal to Palisades Road. Turn right onto Palisades Road, right onto El Portal Drive, and right onto Indio Drive back to the parking lot.

For a more challenging hike (and absolutely without stroller), walk away from the bluff parking lot and cross Indio Drive. Follow the fire access road that runs somewhat parallel to El Portal Drive and watch for the trail to the left just before the fire road turns to dirt. Follow this gentle climb along the foothill toward the freeway, then as it curves more steeply toward the ridge. At the ridge, turn left toward the ocean and continue along the ridge for spectacular views and wonderful displays of native wildflowers in season.

Dinosaur Caves Park
Off Price Street at Cliff Ave.
(805) 773-7039
FREE!

From Highway 101 take the Spyglass Drive exit and turn west. Turn left onto Shell Beach Road, then right onto Cliff Avenue.

The first thing many wonder about Dinosaur Caves is: Where's the dinosaur?

The 11-acre open space on Shell Beach Road known as Dinosaur Caves Park is easy enough to spot, dinosaur or no dinosaur. It is the first large vacant lot south of Shell Beach and it is usually dotted with locals walking their dogs along the bluffs. Kayakers like cruising the kelp beds and paddling in and out of the caves below.

Local history has it that an amusement park once called this property home. H. Douglas Brown began building a concrete dinosaur here in 1948, but never finished due to public outcry. The headless behemoth was removed in the 1950s.

The 11-acre lot with the million-dollar views from above and sea caves below is the city's newest seaside park. Topside, Dinosaur Caves offers wonderful views and wildlife too. Regular sightings include squirrels, rabbits, ducks and myriad birds, sea lions, dolphins, otters, and pelicans. The park includes public restrooms, a playground, trails and lawn. Final plans for this park in transition include two gazebos, an observation telescope, an amphitheatre with its own natural seating area, a learning center and a fishing platform in the cove at the bottom of the bluff. The park is also home to Art in the Park, a public display of local artisans, on the first Sunday of the months May through October.

Some of the best views from Dinosaur Caves Park are underground. Those with the sea in their blood, or perhaps just an adventurous streak will find

Dinosaur Caves Park the perfect spot. The surf has cut caves into the bluffs below the park and kayakers regularly tour the holes as well as the kelp beds just beyond the surf line.

The bluff beyond the fence is unstable, so hikers are strongly advised to heed posted warnings and remain on stable ground.

Ebbtide Park
Off Ebb Tide Court
(805) 773-7039
FREE!

From Highway 101 take the Spyglass Drive exit and turn west. Turn right onto Shell Beach Road, then left onto Ebb Tide Way which ends at the park.

Like most of the parks in Pismo Beach and Shell Beach, Ebbtide Park offers stupendous views of the Pacific coast. The bluff-top park is limited to a grassy area and paved pathway.

Eldwayen Ocean Park
Ocean Boulevard between Palomar and Vista del Mar
(805) 773-7039
FREE!

From Highway 101 take the Spyglass Drive exit and turn west. Turn left onto Shell Beach Road, then right onto Vista del Mar which leads directly to the park.

This is the cove about which locals don't want to tell you. Benches, picnic tables and barbecues sit atop the bluff. Stairs lead down to a lovely cove often visited by seals and otters. This is a popular dog-walking beach for residents and includes both sandy stretches and tide pools.

Many of the parks in SHELL BEACH are located atop bluffs that drop abruptly into the ocean. Keep close tabs on little ones.

Margo Dodd Park

Western end of Cliff Avenue at Ocean Boulevard

(805) 773-7039

FREE!

From Highway 101 take the Spyglass Drive exit and turn west. Turn left onto Shell Beach Road, then right onto Cliff Avenue.

This tiny bluff-top park is most famous for its gazebo and views. Kids enjoy dancing in the gazebo, running on the grass, and checking out the hundreds of pelicans that often roost on the neighboring bluff isolated from the mainland by some 20 yards of ocean.

Memory Park

Seacliff Drive & Baker Avenue

(805) 773-7039

FREE!

From Highway 101 take the Spyglass Drive exit and turn west. Turn left onto Shell Beach Road, then right onto Seacliff Drive which leads directly to the park.

Another bluff-top park with a well-maintained lawn, benches, picnic tables and extremely treacherous access to a small cove. Sea walls protect cliff-top homes from erosion and detract from the beauty of this cove.

Naomi View Platform

Access at Seacliff Drive & Naomi Street

(805) 773-7039

FREE!

From Highway 101 take the Spyglass Drive exit and turn west. Turn left onto Shell Beach Road, then right onto Seacliff Drive and continue past Memory Park.

A narrow public pathway leads to a platform with views of the Pacific.

Palisades Park

Shell Beach Road at Encanto Ave.

(805) 773-7039

FREE!

From Highway 101 take the Avila Beach Drive exit west. From the south, cross under the freeway, and then turn left onto Shell Beach Road. From the north, continue straight off the end of the exit ramp and onto Shell Beach Road.

This 6-acre neighborhood park includes basketball courts, tennis courts, play structures, plenty of room to run on the grass, and picnic areas complete with barbecues.

Palisades Park – South
Indio Drive/Beachcomber Drive/Silver Shoals Drive
(805) 773-7039
FREE!

From Highway 101 take the Avila Beach Drive exit west. From the south, cross under the freeway, and then turn left onto Shell Beach Road. From the north, continue straight off the end of the exit ramp and onto Shell Beach Road. Turn right onto Beachcomber drive or Silver Shoals Drive.

The bluff-top park includes paved pathways and access to the coves below via often sketchy trails. From the end of Beachcomber Drive, follow the cliff trail down to the tide pools.

At low tide, this stretch of sand passes below Ebbtide Park and connects with the Silver Shoals public access stairway at The Cliffs Resort. Silver Shoals is a popular local surfing spot known for its glassy conditions, though it also offers plenty of rock hazards and kelp.

Shell Beach Playground
At Shell Beach Elementary School, 2100 Shell Beach Road
(805) 773-7039
FREE!

From Highway 101 take the Spyglass Drive exit and turn west. Turn left onto Shell Beach Road.

The playground and playing fields at this 4-acre park are available to the general public after school, on weekends and holidays.

Silver Shoals
Access from 2757 Shell Beach Road
(805) 773-7039
FREE!

From Highway 101 take the Spyglass Drive exit and turn west. Turn right onto Shell Beach Road.

This long, sandy cove runs from a public access stairway at The Cliffs Resort all the way north

Take the long climb to the top of the ridge above El Portal Drive to catch this view.

toward Beachcomber Cove. This area is very popular among local surfers and is often referred to as "St. An's" or "St. Andrews."

Park in the public access spots at The Cliffs, and then follow the dirt pathway along the north side of the hotel and down the stairs to the beach.

Spyglass Park
Spyglass Drive & Solano Road
(805) 773-7039
FREE!

From Highway 101 take the Spyglass Drive exit and turn west to the park.
This 4½-acre park with a view of the ocean includes plenty of grass and play structures. There is beach access via a hazardous bluff trail down a ravine to what can, at times, be a tiny rocky cove. At low tide, the beach offers nearly a mile of sand and tide pooling opportunities. It is also popular among local surfers for winter surf.

Thousand Stairsteps
Ocean Blvd. north of Margo Dodd Park
(805) 773-7039
☛ FREE!

From Highway 101 take the Spyglass Drive exit and turn west. Turn left onto Shell Beach Road, then right onto Cliff Avenue and right onto Ocean Boulevard.
This rugged outcropping at the end of Palisade Avenue provides great sound effects, scenery and some protection for the sandy beach and its tide pools. Access is via steep stairs and the beach diminishes as the tide rises.

PISMO PIER is a big draw on holiday weekends and throughout the summer months. But the best weather is typically in the fall when coastal fog and valley tourists both disappear for the season.

Chapter 4

Pismo Beach

The greatest draw at Pismo Beach is its namesake stretch of gently sloping sand and its curvaceous waves. Where the sand stops, beautiful bluffs shelter contemplative coves, secret dynamic tide pools and provide scenic trails.

Perhaps more than anything else, Pismo Beach is about getting outside and making the most of all that the ocean and temperate climate provide. Popular activities here include kayaking, cycling, clamming, fishing, surfing, body boarding, kite surfing and paragliding. Check local phone books for current businesses that provide the necessary equipment and instruction. There is also a plethora of parks from bluff perches to inland historical venues. All parks in Pismo Beach are free and open during daylight hours. Many include picnic/barbecue areas and some have large group areas available by reservation.

NATURE

Boosinger Park
Wadsworth Avenue at Lemoore Avenue
(805) 773-7039
FREE!
From southbound Highway 101 take the Price Street exit. Turn left onto Price Street, left onto Bello Street and right onto Wadsworth Avenue. From northbound Highway 101 take the Wadsworth exit and turn right onto Wadsworth Avenue.

This small neighborhood park offers sweeping 180-degree views of the coast. Amenities include play structures, drinking fountain, picnic tables, barbecues and benches. Come for the park; stay for the view.

Chumash Park
Off Ventana Drive near James Way
(805) 773-7039
☞ FREE!
From Highway 101 turn east onto Fourth Street, left onto James Way, then right onto Ventana Drive.

A 38-acre park that emphasizes its natural setting. Though there are fun play structures here, the park also includes a trail system along wetlands, through oaks and up a beautiful little valley. Nice spot for spring wildflower viewing, catching frogs and meandering.

Cottage Inn Public Access
Access trails and beach via Cottage Inn By The Sea
2351 Price Street
(805) 773-7039
FREE!

From Highway 101 take Mattie Road west to Price Street/Highway 1 south.

Public bluff-top trails give way to miles upon miles of sand and surf. This public throughway on hotel property provides the northernmost access to the long stretch of sand that extends south into Santa Barbara County.

Elmer Ross Beach
Access via trail and stairs behind Shelter Cove Lodge, 2651 Price Street
(805) 773-7039
FREE!

From Highway 101 take Mattie Road west to Price Street/Highway 1 north.

This lesser-known beach, unlike many of its local counterparts, faces west. A large cliff at the southern end of the cove blocks sun from a significant portion of the cove at times. The peaceful little beach here is a treasure. It is also referred to as Shelter Cove.

Highland Park
Highland Drive at Whitecap Street
(805) 773-7039
FREE!

From Highway 101 turn east onto Fourth Street, left onto James Way, then right onto Highland Drive.

This lesser-known 7-acre gem includes play structures and picnic areas in a quiet neighborhood.

Some of Pismo's parks are great spots for catching frogs.

Ira Lease Park
East of Highway 1 at Addie Street
(805) 773-7039
FREE!

From northbound Highway 101 take the Price Street exit. Turn left onto Stimson Avenue, and then left onto South Dolliver / Highway 1.
This 1-acre park includes a creek-side trail, picnic areas and an expanse of grass.

Mary Herrington Park
West of Highway 1 at Addie Street
(805) 773-7039
FREE!

From northbound Highway 101 take the Price Street exit. Turn left onto Stimson Avenue, and then left onto South Dolliver / Highway 1.
A 1-acre park with restroom and grassy stretch along the creek.

Monarch Butterfly Grove
Pismo State Beach
Highway 1 north of Le Sage Drive
(805) 443-7778
www.monarchbutterfly.org/grove.htm
☞ FREE!

From Highway 101 take the Price Street exit. From the north, continue straight from the off ramp onto Dolliver Street / Highway 1. From the south, follow Price Street straight from the off ramp. Turn left onto Ocean View or Stimson avenues, and then left onto Dolliver Street / Highway 1. The grove is on the right south of North Beach Campground.
Every winter some 100,000 Monarch butterflies make this eucalyptus grove home. They float through the air, often landing on or near visitors. Docents who staff the area from 10 a.m. to 4 p.m. daily during butterfly season ask that no one touch the butterflies as doing so can permanently damage their wings. Instead, take binoculars (or use some on site provided by friends of the park), a camera, a jacket and a picnic. This is an ideal spot for a field trip lesson about lifecycles, metamorphosis and migration.

Pismo Beach Pier, Promenade and Park
West end of Pomeroy Avenue
www.pismobeach.org
☞ FREE!

From Highway 101 take the Price Street exit. From the north, continue straight from the off ramp onto Dolliver Street / Highway 1, turn right onto Pomeroy Avenue. From the south, follow Price Street straight from the off ramp. Turn left onto Pomeroy Avenue.

This 60-acre public beach is highlighted by its photogenic pier, classic swings, sand volleyball courts and the new addition of the Pismo Beach Promenade.

For more than 125 years a public pier has offered Pismo Beach visitors and locals alike a place to fish, walk, dance, dine, and peer down on shapely waves. Though storms have wreaked havoc on the pier, local authorities have rebuilt it bigger and better than before. Today the 1,370-foot icon remains a popular spot for fishing since it provides great access beyond the surf line (check out the fishing decks down the stairs near the west end of the pier) and fishing permits are not required. Top catches include perch, skates, halibut, jack smelt and flounder.

During the winter holiday season, the city erects a tree of lights at the end of the pier. On July Fourth the pier serves as the launching pad for the city's fireworks extravaganza. A variety of festivals are centered on the pier as are private fetes like weddings and reunions. The pier is lighted every night throughout the year, providing just enough light for night surfers and shark fishing.

Not a day goes by that surfers can't be found in the water below the pier. Most seem to enjoy the combination of a high tide and gentle breeze so if your key interest here is observing surfers or taking to the waves yourself, watch for these conditions.

According to the city, a million and a half people visit the pier every year. In recent years the city has expanded the base facilities to include a 550-foot first phase boardwalk that will eventually stretch from the pier to Grand Avenue in Grover Beach. The Pismo Beach Promenade is designed to match

the Pismo Beach Municipal Fishing Pier which stretches into the Pacific Ocean about 40 yards further north. Benches are strategically placed off the 15-foot-wide pathway to provide rest and views. Half-round lights reminiscent of ship deck lights are mounted midway up the promenade banisters to continue the ocean theme.

Other facilities at the base of the pier include a public restroom with cold showers, free parking, fish-cleaning stations, benches and picnic tables. Local businesses provide a variety of dining and shopping opportunities nearby. Public volleyball nets stretch across the sand for pickup games and occasional organized events. Nearby old-style swings offer rides to children and children at heart.

Pismo Beach Sports Complex
East end of Frady Lane
(805) 773-7039
FREE!

From southbound Highway 101 take the Hinds Avenue exit. Turn right onto Hinds Avenue, left onto Price Street, right onto Stimson, then left onto South Dolliver/Highway 1 before finally turning left onto Frady Lane. From northbound Highway 101 take the 4th Street exit and head south into Grover Beach. Turn right onto Grand Avenue, then right onto Highway 1, and then right onto Frady Lane.

Used largely for organized athletic events for all ages, this park includes baseball fields, picnic areas and public restrooms.

Pismo Lake Ecological Preserve
Off Fourth Street west of Highway 101
(805) 773-7039
FREE!

From Highway 101 take the Fourth Street exit. Turn south onto Fourth Street.

The 69-acre preserve consists of 30-acres of lakes that host myriad plant and animal life surrounded by a sea of humanity. Access to the preserve is limited to foot traffic. There are no trail systems or maintained viewpoints, but an observation platform, an interpretive center, trails and a docent guide program are in the works.

Pismo State Beach North Beach Campground
555 Pier Ave.
(805) 489-2684
www.parks.ca.gov
$$

From Highway 101 take the Price Street exit. From the north, continue straight from the off ramp onto Dolliver Street/Highway 1. From the south, follow Price Street straight from the off ramp. Turn left onto Ocean View or

Stimson avenues, and then left onto Dolliver Street/Highway 1. The
campground is on the right.

This campground is separated from the Pacific Ocean only by a band of
beach and foredunes. The 103 sites are developed. Reservations highly
suggested.

Price Historical Park
580 Frady Lane
(805) 473-0563
FREE!-$

From Highway 101 take the Price Street exit. From the north, continue
straight from the off ramp onto Dolliver Street/Highway 1, turn left onto
Price Canyon Road, right onto Bello Street and right onto Frady Lane. From
the south, follow Price Street straight from the off ramp. Turn right onto
Price Canyon Road, right onto Bello Street and right onto Frady Lane.

This 40-acre historical museum park has been in the works for three
decades. Once completed, it is slated to include historic residences
emphasizing the life and times of Rancho Pismo,the John Michael Price
family, and the Chumash who lived here before them. Plans also call for
rock corral replicas, restoration of the Price Anniversary House built here in
1893, restoration of adobe structures on the site, a theater in an orchard,
and a barn.

Open 11 a.m. to 3 p.m. on the first and third Sundays of each month.

Shore Cliff Lodge Beach Access
Access via spiral staircase behind Shore Cliff Lodge, 2555
Price Street
(805) 773-7039
FREE!

From Highway 101 take the Mattie Road exit. Turn west onto Mattie Road,
then left onto Price Street.

Follow the spiral staircase for public access to this little known cove.

Wilmar Steps
Oceanic end of Wilmar Avenue
(805) 773-7039
FREE!

From Highway 101 take the Mattie Road exit. Turn west onto Mattie Road,
then left onto Price Street, then right onto Wilmar Avenue.

A long, steep set of stairs provides neighbors and visitors access to the
lesser-visited northwestern end of Pismo Beach. Only a hop and skip from
the Cottage Inn Public Access and bluff-top trails.

OTHER ADVENTURES

Pismo Bowl
277 Pomeroy Ave.
(805) 773-2482
www.pismobowl.com

☛ $

From Highway 101 take the Price Street exit. From the north, continue straight from the off ramp onto Dolliver Street/Highway 1, turn right onto Pomeroy Avenue. From the south, follow Price Street straight from the off ramp. Turn left onto Pomeroy Avenue.

Not every bowling alley serves as a destination, but this family-owned and operated eight-lane throwback is nostalgic and fun for people of any age. Real wooden lanes may not be plum, but with the help of gutter bumpers, the kids are unlikely to notice.

While bowling alleys across the nation have suffered from decreased interest, Pismo Bowl continues to hop not only with league play for all ages and abilities, but also theme nights. Cosmic Bowling is one of those unusual events designed to attract an energetic crowd. The weekly Friday night event involves loud music, fog, blacklights, and strobes from 9 p.m. to midnight. The alley also offers a junior bowling league every Saturday from 9:45 a.m. to noon for bowlers ages 6 to 21. Junior league play includes instruction and

competition. Evening leagues offer those over 21 some alley time and senior leagues are held weekdays.

Bowling amenities also include automatic scoring, shoe rentals and ball rentals. Other activities here include billiards, video games, a pro shop, and a grill.

Chapter 5

Grover Beach

City namesake Dwight William Grover dreamed this coastal town would become a tourist center and transit hub. More than 110 years later, the 2.25-square-mile city has become instead a haven for families seeking relatively affordable homes in a safe, friendly coastal community. Its lack of major attractions and major events attest to the small-town mentality of city officials and residents while contributing to this city's charm.

Grover Beach is rife with thrift shops, junk shops, and treasure shops. It also hosts a diverse range of restaurants featuring seafood to Mexican food, pizza to sushi.

The largest influx of visitors these days is headed for California's only remaining drive-on beach: Oceano Dunes State Vehicular Recreation Area. According to California State Parks, 1.5 million visitors pass the kiosks to play in the sand with a variety of off-highway vehicles, family vehicles, RVs and campers. Most of those enter at Grover Beach's Grand Avenue ramp.

For those who want a quieter visit with nature, Grover Beach offers a pedestrian boardwalk through the dunes. The wooden walkway leads visitors away from the roar of engines toward the whisper of wings half a mile north at the Monarch butterfly grove in neighboring Pismo Beach.

LETTERS

Grover Beach Community Library
867 Ramona Avenue

(805) 473-1421

FREE!

From Highway 101 take 4ᵗʰ Street south, turn left onto Atlantic City Avenue, right onto 9ᵗʰ Street and right onto Ramona Avenue.

This very small, non-profit library operates outside the county library system. It focuses on the needs of community youth and seniors. The library shares the building with Central Coast Exploration Station.

NATURE

16th Street Park

On 16th Street between Nice and Mentone avenues

(805) 473-4580

www.grover.org/gr_pr.htm

FREE!

From Highway 101 take Oak Park Boulevard south. Turn right onto Mentone Avenue.

The park includes a play structure, running room, covered group barbecue area, horseshoe pits, softball field and a grass volleyball court.

Costa Bella Park

Corner of Oak Park Blvd. and Farroll Ave.

(805) 473-4580

www.grover.org/gr_pr.htm

FREE!

From Highway 101 take Oak Park Boulevard south to Farroll Avenue.

This grassy park on the corner has become a popular spot for locals to walk their dogs. Do not bring children here if they are uncomfortable with dogs. Beware that some dogs can be unpredictable and dangerous. Cleanup bags are available for those who opt to stretch their pets here.

Golden West Park

At the end of Jennifer Court

(805) 473-4580

www.grover.org/gr_pr.htm

FREE!

From Highway 101 take Oak Park Boulevard south. Turn right onto The Pike, right onto Lynn Street and right onto Jennifer Court.

This pocket park offers a bit of room to run, picnic tables, horseshoe pit and barbecues.

Grover Heights Park

Atlantic City Avenue at the end of North 9th Street

(805) 473-4580

www.grover.org/gr_pr.htm
FREE!
From Highway 101 take 4th Street south, turn left onto Atlantic City Avenue.

Lots of room to run, climb play structures and host a barbecue. The park includes horseshoe pits, barbecues, sand volleyball court, basketball court and lighted tennis courts.

Hero Community Park

Farroll Ave at South 16th Street

(805) 473-4580

www.grover.org/gr_pr.htm

☛ FREE!

From Highway 101 take Oak Park Boulevard south. Turn right onto Farroll Avenue.

The city's newest park, named for the family that owned a hog farm near this site, features ocean-themed play structures and some of the coolest new equipment around. While other citics lay waste to the age-old favorite merry-go-round, Grover Beach has added a new mini version that offers great physics lessons. Ask standing riders to huddle together toward the center post. Get them spinning, and then tell them to hold tight while they lean out simultaneously for an unexpected boost. The park also includes a basketball court, tennis court, horseshoe pits, barbecue areas and restroom.

Mentone Basin Park

Mentone Ave. between south 14th and 16th streets

(805) 473-4580

www.grover.org/gr_pr.htm

FREE!

From Highway 101 take Oak Park Boulevard south. Turn right onto Mentone Avenue.

This large grassy park also has barbecue areas, and lighted basketball and tennis courts.

Ramona Garden Park

900 block of Ramona Ave.

(805) 473-4580

www.grover.org/gr_pr.htm

FREE!

From Highway 101 take 4th Street south, turn left onto Atlantic City Avenue, right onto 9th Street.

Features a gazebo, restroom, Ramona Garden Park Center (capacity 438 standing, 251 seated), an amphitheatre and grass for free roamers. It's a popular park for events like the city's annual Stone Soup Festival.

South County Skate Park

1750 Ramona Ave.

(805) 473-4580

www.grover.org/skatepark.htm

$

From Highway 101 take Oak Park Boulevard south, turn right onto Ramona Avenue.

This 13,234-square-foot park features pool-style action for inline skating and skateboards only. (No bicycles allowed.) The park is staffed by city parks employees and hosts special events throughout the year. Helmets, knee pads and elbow pads are required and are available for free one-day rentals.

OTHER ADVENTURES

Pismo State Golf Course

25 Grand Avenue

(805) 473-3467

www.pismogolf.com

$

From Highway 101 take 4th Street exit and head south. Turn right onto Grand Avenue.

This public 9-hole three par course is open 365 days per year from sunup to sundown. The putting and pitching green, water hazards, greens and roughs are one slice away from the dunes and only a few good swings from the Pacific Ocean.

Central Coast Exploration Station

867 Ramona Avenue

(805) 473-1421

home.kcbx.net/~estation

$

From Highway 101 take 4th Street south, turn left onto Atlantic City Avenue, right onto 9th Street and right onto Ramona Avenue.

This educational center in the city's old fire station offers a variety of classes designed for and about children. The center features a 350-gallon aquarium and rotating exhibits. Expansion of this relatively new endeavor is in the works. Future plans include a firefighters' museum and an arts and crafts center. The venue shares the building with Grover Beach Community Library.

The Village of Arroyo Grande is historic and quaint with locally owned shops and more than half a dozen restaurants, but Arroyo Grande also serves as a gateway to the LOS PADRES NATIONAL FOREST. The back country includes a variety of hiking, horseback riding, mule packing, mountain biking and off-highway-vehicle opportunities, campgrounds and a California condor monitoring station housed in an old fire lookout.

Chapter 6

Arroyo Grande

Arroyo Grande's translation to English "big ditch" doesn't do this Central Coast city justice. This valley 2 miles from the Pacific Ocean charmed even its earliest European settler, Francisco Zeba Branch, with its wild beauty. Today the city invites visitors interested in browsing, dining, picnicking and antiquing.

Branch acquired nearly 17,000 acres in the Arroyo Grande Valley after his first visit in 1832. His cattle dominated the land until 1864 when drought forced him to sell parcels to settlers.

"By 1876, there were 35 families and the farm-based community began to flourish," the city of Arroyo Grande reports. "A railway depot was established in 1882. In 1911 residents voted to incorporate the city of Arroyo Grande. From the beginning businesses were established along a road appropriately named Branch Street."

Nearly a century later that original shopping area remains the commercial and governmental hub of the city and is commonly called the Arroyo Grande Village. Residential neighborhoods stretch up Crown Hill, over neighboring hill and dale and west onto the flatlands.

The city's namesake "big ditch" also remains a central feature of the village. Heavy winter storms can turn Arroyo Grande Creek into a muddy, boiling rivulet, but most days it's an inviting trickle of water that generally divides the city's commercial district from its quiet old-town neighborhood.

ARTS

Clark Center for the Performing Arts
Arroyo Grande High School
(805) 489-9444
www.clarkcenter.org
Prices vary
From northbound Highway 101 take the Traffic Way exit and proceed straight toward town, then turn left onto Fair Oaks Avenue. From southbound Highway 101 take the Grand Avenue/Branch Street exit, turn east onto Branch Street, right onto Traffic Way, and then right onto Fair Oaks Avenue.

This theater, owned and operated by the Lucia Mar Unified School District, was built after a huge fundraising effort by local volunteers. It serves as a venue for local and international performers in one of two theaters: the 600-seat Forbes Hall and the 150 studio theater. Rules involving children are very strict. Check at the box office IN PERSON before purchasing any tickets for children. Children are banned from some shows, and even babes in arms are required to have tickets.

Fair Oaks Theatre
1007 E. Grand Ave.
(805) 489-2364
$$
From Highway 101 take the Grand Avenue exit and head west.
Known locally as the "dollar theater," Fair Oaks offers cheap seats (though no longer just a buck) for first run movies that are a little behind the times. If you missed it at the blockbuster theater but still want to catch it on the big screen, this is the place.

Signature Theatres Festival Cinemas
1160 W. Branch St.
(805) 481-7553
$$
From northbound Highway 101 take the Oak Park Road exit. Turn right at the end of the ramp onto West Branch Street.
Stadium seating at this 10-screen theater may make it more attractive to the shorter set. The marquee regularly emphasizes Hollywood blockbusters.

LETTERS

Arroyo Grande Library
800 W. Branch St.
(805) 473-7161
www.slolibrary.org
FREE!
From Highway 101 take the Grand Avenue/Branch Street exit. Turn east onto Branch Street, then immediately left onto West Branch Street. The Library is in the South County Regional Center on the right side of the road.
This branch of the San Luis Obispo City/County Library system features an expansive children's section and weekly preschool story time.

Doc Burnstein's Ice Cream Factory
114 W. Branch Street
(805) 474-4068
www.docburnsteins.com
FREE!
From Highway 101 take the Grand Avenue exit and turn east. (Grand Avenue becomes Branch Street as it passes through the downtown area immediately east of the freeway.)
Besides offering homemade ice cream, this shop in the Arroyo Grande Village welcomes visitors to watch the ice cream making process and attend

special events. Doc's Reading Lab, held every Tuesday from 3:30 p.m. to 4:15 p.m., is a free public reading event designed for young children.

HISTORY

Heritage House Museum
126 Mason St.
(805) 473-5077
www.southcountyshistory.org
☛ FREE!

From Highway 101 take the Grand Avenue exit and turn east, then turn right onto Mason Street.

This home, built in the late 1800s, has served in a variety of capacities as a single-family residence, duplex, Dr. Walter's Sanatorium, city daycare facility, and home to the city's parks and recreation department. Now completely renovated, the house serves as a visitors center and a museum including all sorts of interesting local artifacts including period clothing, photographs and household items. Be sure to continue out the back door to the barn with its antique tractors, agriculture equipment, a gazebo and gardens.

Open Saturdays noon to 3 p.m. and Sundays 1 p.m. to 4 p.m.

Paulding House
551 Crown Hill Road
(805) 473-5077
www.southcountyhistory.org
FREE!

From Highway 101 take the Grand Avenue/Branch Street exit. Turn east onto Branch Street. Where Branch Street curves right around Crown Hill, take the lesser-traveled street straight ahead, Crown Hill Road.

Docents offer guided tours of this home by appointment and on the first Saturday of each month from noon to 3 p.m.

A 250-year-old oak tree spans the front yard of this historic home which housed the city's first resident physician. In 1891, Dr. Edwin Paulding bought the two-year-old house in which he and his family made their home until donating it, along with all its contents, to the South County Historical Society in 1998. Artifacts include carvings made by Dr. Paulding and authentic Chumash Indian basketry.

Santa Manuela Schoolhouse
127 Short Street
(805) 473-5077
www.southcountyhistory.org
FREE!

From Highway 101 take the Grand Avenue/Branch Street exit. Turn east onto Branch Street, turn left onto Short Street.

This one-room schoolhouse was built in 1901 on property that is now under Lopez Lake. After 56 years as a school, two moves and a renovation, the structure now serves as home to South County Historical Society. The building and grounds are open for free tours Saturdays from noon to 3 p.m. and Sundays 1 p.m. to 4 p.m.

The grounds also include the barn annex which houses historic vehicles and other machinery, Heritage House, gazebo and gardens.

NATURE

Biddle Regional Park
3500 Lopez Drive
(805) 781-5930
FREE!-$

From Highway 101 take the Grand Avenue/Branch Street exit. Turn east onto Branch Street and follow it as it curves around Crown Hill. Turn right onto Huasna Road which becomes Lopez Drive. Continue about 5 miles.

This county day-use park includes playgrounds, ball fields, picnic areas and plenty of running room. An entrance fee is charged when the kiosk is staffed.

Community Garden
1221 Ash Street
(805) 473-5474
FREE!-$

From Highway 101 take Oak Park Boulevard south, turn left onto Ash Street.

These public gardens are available for rent from the city on a first-come, first-served basis. Walk through for a quick garden lesson or rent a plot of your own for thorough education.

Cypress Ridge Golf Resort
780 Cypress Ridge Parkway
(805) 474-7979
www.cypressridge.com
$$$

From Highway 101 take Grand Avenue west, turn left onto Halcyon Road, left onto Highway 1/Cienaga Street which becomes Mesa View Drive. Turn left onto Halcyon Road (again), right onto West El Campo Road and then left onto Cypress Ridge Parkway.

Cypress Ridge's 18-hole Peter Jacobsen course has been designated a signature sanctuary by Audubon International. The course is unique in its ability to enhance habitat and conserve wildlife but is in no way designed for junior golfers. This is a spot for budding champions with well-established skills.

Elm Street Park
350 S. Elm Street
(805) 473-5474
FREE!

From Highway 101 take the Grand Avenue/Branch Street exit. Turn west onto Grand Avenue and then left onto Elm Street.

This park next to the Soto Sports Complex includes volleyball standards, large grass area, barbecue area, restrooms and nautical-themed play structures.

Hart-Collett Memorial Park
Traffic Way and Bridge Street
(805) 473-5474
FREE!

From Highway 101 take the Grand Avenue/Branch Street exit. Turn east onto Branch Street, and then right onto Traffic Way.

Possibly the smallest park in the county, this triangular bit of grass surrounded by busy streets is dedicated to the memory of Harry Hart and Robert "Bob" Collett who were both long-time firefighters for the Arroyo Grande Fire Department. The park includes picnic tables and benches, grass and flowerbeds shaded by trees.

Health Fitness Park
Fair Oaks Avenue near Woodland Drive
(805) 473-5474
FREE!

From Highway 101 take the Grand Avenue exit. Turn west onto Grand Avenue, left onto Halcyon Road and then left onto Fair Oaks Avenue.

A paved pathway leads visitors through a variety of exercise stations tucked between the back of Arroyo Grande Community Hospital and Arroyo Grande Creek.

Hoosegow Park
Le Point Street
(805) 473-5474
FREE!

From Highway 101 take the Grand Avenue/Branch Street exit. Turn east onto Branch Street, left onto Nevada Street, then follow the curve to the right onto LePoint Street.

This pocket park overlooking Arroyo Grande Village is named for the tiny old city jail, built around 1910 and still standing (though usually vacant).

James Way Oak Habitat and Wildlife Preserve

James Way between La Canada and Stevenson Drive

(805) 473-5474

☞ FREE!

From Highway 101 take Oak Park Boulevard east. Turn right onto James Way. The preserve is on the right.

This nature preserve seems unlikely as motorists quickly pass from shopping area to residential development, but the preserve offers a fantastic reprieve from all things city. Maintained trails lead through old growth oak forests where deer, fox, bobcats, rabbits and myriad birds are often seen. The windmill, water tank and surrounding garden are highlights.

Kingo Park

Courtland Street

(805) 473-5474

FREE!

From Highway 101 take Oak Park Boulevard south, turn left onto Ash Street and then turn left onto Courtland Street.

Another neighborhood pocket park with a play structure, picnic tables and barbecue grills.

Kiwanis Park

Kiwanis Park is on the opposite side of the parking lot behind Ira's Bike Shop on Bridge Street.

(805) 473-5474

☞ FREE!

From Highway 101 take the Grand Avenue/Branch Street exit. Turn east onto Branch Street, right onto Bridge Street and left into the first parking lot.

The Bridge Street Bridge offers a good view of the park, and the pathway down is relatively well maintained and easy.

La Mesa Village Park

Bambi Court

(805) 473-5474

FREE!

From Highway 101 take Traffic Way or Fair Oaks Avenue exit. Turn west onto Fair Oaks Avenue, left onto Valley Road, left onto Tiger Tail Drive and then right onto Bambi Court.

This pocket park offers a little room to run.

Lopez Lake Recreation Area

10 miles east of Arroyo Grande on Lopez Lake Drive

(805) 788-2381

www.slocountyparks.com/activities/lopez.htm

LOPEZ LAKE RECREATION AREA offers organized youth fishing days, but youngsters are welcome to fish the planted lake anytime when accompanied by a licensed adult.

$

From Highway 101 take the Grand Avenue/Branch Street exit. Turn east onto Branch Street, right onto Huasna Road which becomes Lopez Drive and continues 10 miles to the lake.

This man-made lake has served as southern San Luis Obispo County's inland recreational mecca for sport fishing, waterskiing, sailing, picnicking, hiking, canoeing and bird watching since 1969. In recent years mountain biking has been added to the list of things to do, as well as taking the plunge at Mustang Water Slides which operates within the park's boundary.

When the lake is completely full, it offers 22 miles of shoreline and nearly 1,000 acres of lake surface. Still mornings make early glass for water skiers while afternoon winds assure a good ride for sailboarders. Regular rainbow trout plants add to other frequent catches which include crappie, red-ear sunfish, bigmouth bass, small mouth bass and catfish. The park sponsors regular fishing days during which children are paired with fishing buddies who offer pointers with loaner rods and reels. The marina includes launch ramp, ample parking, a food market, tackle shop and boat rentals.

The area also includes 354 campsites that vary from primitive to full hook ups for trailers and motor homes. Reservations are advised. Some camp restrooms include hot showers.

More than 15 miles of hiking, biking and equestrian trails are particularly popular during late spring when wildflower blooms peak. Perhaps the easiest hike in the park is the half-mile Marina Trail. It begins just inside the park entrance past the old barn. Another easy option is the 15-minute walk through the oaks out to Rocky Point, a popular fishing spot overlooking the lake's Arroyo Grande Arm. One of the most popular trails among mountain bikers is the Tuoski-Two Waters Trail-Dune Vista Trail loop off the lake's Wittenberg Arm. It features expansive 360-degree views which are particularly striking at sunrise and sunset. Hard-core climbers enjoy Wittenberg Trail which leads up the steep ridge to Hi Ridge Trail.

Visitors with a boat and responsible children might consider boating out the Lopez Arm, dropping their children and an adult guide at the Two Waters Trail, then boating peacefully around to the Wittenberg Arm to pick up the walkers at the trail's end.

For sunbathing, begin exploring the shore at Cove Beach off Grizzly Drive, then venture farther into the park for more privacy.

Los Padres National Forest
Hi Mountain Road east of Arroyo Grande
(805) 925-9538
www.fs.fed.us/r5/lospadres/recreation/wilderness/
www.fs.fed.us/r5/lospadres/
☞ FREE!/$

From Highway 101 take the Grand Avenue/Branch Street exit. Turn east onto Branch Street, right onto Huasna Road which becomes Lopez Drive. Follow the road about 9 miles, then turn right onto Hi Mountain Road which continues 15 miles through private lands and forest and connects with Pozo Road.

The LPNF includes some 1.75 million acres in five counties including expansive holdings east of Arroyo Grande. This area, which is managed by the Santa Lucia Ranger District, includes trails for hikers, bikers, horses and off-highway vehicles and campgrounds.

Local highlights include Hi Mountain Condor Lookout (www.condorlookout.org) on the 3,198-foot crest of Hi Mountain Ridge. The old fire lookout has been transformed into a field research station that is

staffed full-time in summer by student biologists who track the endangered California condor. The project, supported by the Morro Coast Audubon Society, U.S. Forest Service, U.S. Fish and Wildlife Service, Ventana Wilderness Society and Cal Poly Biological Sciences

Department, features a small interpretive center and expansive views over condor territory.

Garcia Ridge (junction Hi Mountain Road) is an off-highway-vehicle access road that offers 360-degree views that span from the Pacific Ocean to Sierra Nevada Range. Experienced mountain bikers may enjoy this ride along the eastern ridge in late fall, winter or spring, but summer jaunts are not advised due to high heat. There is a picnic table near Balm of Gilead where a barricade blocks motorized vehicles. The old road otherwise offers nice travel.

Hi Mountain Lookout Road (junction Hi Mountain Road) is a graded dirt road generally passable by street-legal vehicles. It leads to Hi Mountain Campground, a primitive area that includes pit toilets but no running water, on to the condor lookout, and west along the ridge with its spectacular views. The 6-mile road ends abruptly after passing several abandoned mines and the Big Falls and Little Falls trailheads.

Rancho Grande Park

500 block of James Way

(805) 473-5474

FREE!

From Highway 101 take Oak Park Road east, turn right onto James Way.

This large neighborhood park includes two play structures, a basketball court, horseshoe pits, barbecue areas and open grass.

Santa Lucia Wilderness

East of Arroyo Grande off Lopez Lake Drive

(805) 925-9538

www.fs.fed.us/r5/lospadres/recreation/wilderness/

☞ FREE!/$

From Highway 101 take the Grand Avenue/Branch Street exit. Turn east onto Branch Street, right onto Huasna Road which becomes Lopez Drive. Follow the road about 9 miles, then turn right onto Hi Mountain Road.

Since 1978 this 20,412-acre wilderness in Los Padres National Forest has provided recreational opportunities that today include hiking, camping, mountain biking and equestrian use.

There are already a number of fantastic books outlining trails in this area. See Resources at the end of this book.

Two local favorites in this expansive area include Big Falls (Upper Lopez Canyon, 9 miles from Hi Mountain Road) and Little Falls (Upper Lopez Canyon, 13.5 miles from Hi Mountain Road).

Because the falls are located in the wilderness, trail travel is limited to equestrian and foot traffic. But the road in from the end of the pavement to the trailheads makes a great mountain bike ride for experienced riders. This section of graded dirt road features multiple creek crossings which may be impassable during winter storm season or, for low-clearance vehicles, at any time of year.

Hiking the BIG FALLS TRAIL loop is no small feat. Only fit hikers are likely to make the loop. But the trail is equally enjoyable as an out-and-back adventure.

Hike either of the two trails as they meander back and forth across year-round streams. Little Falls Creek offers cascades and some small falls. Big Falls Creek is just as its name implies. Swimming holes abound on both. (Do not swim under waterfalls. Debris varying in size from leaves to large boulders can and will fall from above at any time.)

Each hike can be done independently, but they make a great loop hike. Start at the Little Falls trailhead, hike 2.6 miles to Hi Mountain Lookout Road. Turn left at the graded dirt road and follow it about 2 miles. Near the road's end, the Big Falls Trailhead takes off to the RIGHT. Follow that trail 2.6 miles down to Upper Lopez Canyon Road for a 4-mile return along the graded dirt road and several more creek crossings.

Soto Sports Complex

1275 Ash Street

(805) 473-5474

FREE!

From Highway 101 take Oak Park Boulevard south, turn left onto Ash Street.

This large athletic park includes lighted ball fields, tennis courts, and field sports facilities.

Strother Community Park

1150 Huasna Road

(805) 473-5474

☛ FREE!

From Highway 101 take the Grand Avenue/Branch Street exit. Turn east onto Branch Street and follow it as it curves around Crown Hill. Turn right onto Huasna Road.

Among the most family-friendly parks in the city, Strother Park includes play structures, a ball field, basketball court, grass volleyball court and picnic areas, three large picnic areas adequate for moderately sized groups, restrooms and horseshoe pits. The park extends down to Arroyo Grande Creek.

Terra de Oro Park

311 Oro Drive

(805) 473-5474

FREE!

From Highway 101 take the Grand Avenue/Branch Street exit. Turn east onto Branch Street and follow it as it curves around Crown Hill. Turn right onto Huasna Road, and then left onto Oro Drive.

This small neighborhood park that has no restroom but does include play structures and volleyball standards.

Village Green Gazebo, Gazebo Park and Swinging Bridge

Olohan Alley and Short Street, directly behind City Hall

(805) 473-5474

☛ FREE!

From Highway 101 take the Grand Avenue/Branch Street exit. Turn east onto Branch Street, right onto Bridge Street, then left into the first parking lot.

This grassy spot features a picturesque gazebo and the city's historic swinging bridge which offers a clear vantage point for viewing the creek. According to local history, the Short family built the bridge in early 1875 when they owned this section of land divided by the creek. The 171-foot-long bridge is now owned and maintained by the city. City officials are so proud of the bridge, which they claim to be the only one of its kind in California, they issue a wallet-sized "Lifetime Pass to the Swinging Bridge" to any interested party. Send an e-mail, including your mailing address, to Arroyo Grande city staff at agcity@arroyogrande.org to receive a pass and a personal greeting from the mayor.

OTHER ADVENTURES

Bitter Creek Western Railroad

2110 S. Halcyon Road

(805) 481-7353

www.bittercreekwesternrr.org

☛ FREE!

From Highway 101 take the Grand Avenue/Branch Street exit. Turn west onto Grand Avenue, left onto Halcyon Road and follow it out of town.

This private 7.5-inch gauge railroad includes 1.2 miles of mainline with various sidings and two rail yards. Owner/hobbyist Karl Hovanitz maintains the 7-acre site for his entertainment and for the entertainment of his friends, but opens it to the general public on the third Saturday of each month.

Free rides take visitors past a variety of facilities including fourteen steaming bays, a hydraulic lift, turntable, car barn, three bridges, three trestles, four tunnels and six water sources.

Five Cities Swim Club

425 Traffic Way

(805) 481-6399

$-$$$

From southbound Highway 101 take the Fair Oaks exit, turn left at the top of the ramp, then right onto Traffic Way. From northbound Highway 101 take the Traffic Way exit and proceed straight ahead.

This privately owned indoor swimming pool is designed with the very young and very old in mind. The water is always warm, and the windows typically are not vented enough to promote a breeze. There are plentiful toys in this 20-yard pool and a full schedule of recreational swimming, lap swimming, water aerobics as well as individual and small-group lessons. There are no lockers and the dressing room situation is less than ideal. Plan on a quick shower and tight squeeze in small shared space, or plan to shower and change elsewhere.

Mustang Water Slides

Lopez Lake Recreation Area

(805) 489-8898

www.mustangwaterslides.com

$$-$$$

From Highway 101 take the Grand Avenue/Branch Street exit. Turn east onto Branch Street, right onto Huasna Road which becomes Lopez Drive. Follow the road 10 miles east, pay the toll to enter Lopez Lake Recreation Area, and then continue on to the slides.

From May through September the county's oldest waterslide park offers thrills for the entire family. Visitors hike uphill with mats to mount either of the two original slides for a 600-foot, wet, curvy, twisty ride to the final plunge. The addition of Poly Pools and Slides, three mini-slides leading from one wading pool to another, provides thrills for kids 9 and younger. In 2005, the park added Stampede, a 38-foot-tall half pipe. The adventurous hike up stairs for a plunge with up to three riders on a raft.

Four hot tubs provide a more relaxing retreat or a place to warm up between slide runs. The park also includes dressing rooms, lockers, and a snack bar. (No outside food or beverages are permitted, but there are picnic areas directly outside the water slide park.)

Triple T Turtle Ranch/Home for Wayward Turtles and Tortoises
(805) 481-5222

www.tortoise.org

FREE!-$

Call for directions.

A private home that has become just what its name implies. At last count, the five-acre park-like property was home to more than 350 turtles representing more than 50 species. The site is also home to more than 100 birds. One-hour group tours are available by reservation only. Minimum age: 8.

MUSTANG WATER SLIDES in Lopez Lake Recreation Area has modernized and upgraded to include slides and pools for all ages.

Chapter 7

Oceano

Oceano is a community quite literally divided by the railroad tracks. To the west is the beach town, the resort town, a gateway to one of California's last remaining beaches open to motorized vehicles. To the east is a quiet bedroom community with a handful of restaurants, services and a melodramatic holdout.

The town is best known for its access to Oceano Dunes State Vehicular Recreation Area, the last beachfront off-highway recreational vehicle area remaining in California. Some 1 million visitors per year from around the globe, though most from the Central Valley and Southern California, bring motorcycles, quad runners, dune buggies and four-wheel-drive vehicles to the beach to challenge the steep dunes. Some stay in area hotels, but most camp by tent, trailer or recreational vehicle on the sand just a Frisbee toss from the Pacific Ocean.

From the birth of the automobile, people were allowed to drive the length of the beach stretching from Pismo Beach's white cliffs south to Devil's Slide in the Guadalupe-Nipomo Dunes Complex. The area was popular with

picnickers, campers and, in the 1930s and 1940s, a group of freethinking artists, hermits, writers and nudists who referred to themselves as Dunites.

The city of Pismo Beach was first to block motorized traffic from its beaches in an effort to protect pedestrians and the tourist dollars they brought to the city. In 1987, the state fenced vehicles out of the southern 10 miles and 13,500 acres. The move was intended to protect the 1,400 known species of plants and animals living in the unique area.

In more recent years, oceanfront residents in Oceano have persuaded the state to further limit beach access and uses in the 3½-mile stretch of beach marked by numbered posts two through eight. Today the ramps at Pier Avenue in Oceano and Grand Avenue in Grover Beach provide motorists access to 1,500 acres of open sand dunes and beachfront property.

Pedestrians, however, are allowed on the entire stretch of sand, and horseback riding is allowed in many areas. Other area attractions include all-terrain vehicle rentals, biplane rides, and horse rentals for rides on the beach. Check telephone directories for current business listings.

ARTS

Great American Melodrama & Vaudeville Revue
1863 Pacific Blvd. (Highway 1)
(805) 489-2499
www.americanmelodrama.com
☞ $$

From the north, take Highway 101 south to Halcyon Road south 3 miles to its intersection with Highway 1. Turn right onto Highway 1. The melodrama is about 1 ½ miles west. From the south, take Highway 101 to the Los Berros Road/Oceano exit. Turn left onto Los Berros Road, cross under the freeway, then continue 5 miles to its intersection with Valley Road. Turn left onto Valley Road, then right onto Highway 1. The melodrama is about 2 miles west.

For more than 30 years this live theater has offered entertainment. An audience of strangers quickly gets acquainted thanks to cabaret-style seating. Players also serve as hosts and hostesses at the snack bar during intermission as the stage and costumes change from the first show to the ensuing vaudeville review. Unlike so many other area theaters, the melodrama welcomes audience participation in turn-of-the-20th-Century style. Boo as the dark-cloaked villain steals away a fair maiden. Cheer with gusto as her hero returns to save the day. Or will he?

HISTORY

Oceano Railroad Depot/Museum
1650 Front St
(805) 489-5446
FREE!

From Highway 101 take 4th Street south, turn right onto Grand Avenue, left onto Highway 1/Pacific Boulevard which becomes Front Street.

This original Pacific Coast Line depot was built in 1904. It was completely restored prior to celebrating its centennial and today serves as a picturesque railroad museum and community center. The depot/museum is generally open Sundays from 1 p.m. to 4 p.m.

NATURE

Oceano Community Park & Oceano Lagoon

Pier Avenue

(805) 781-5930

www.slocountyparks.com/activities/oceano.htm

FREE!

From Highway 101 take 4th Street south, turn right onto Grand Avenue, left onto Highway 1/Pacific Boulevard and right onto Pier Avenue.

This scenic park is popular for duck feeding and bird watching. Coots have nearly overrun other species of birds here, but provide fine entertainment for kids and may contribute more than their fare share to the lagoon's pungent aroma. New playground equipment across Norswing Street beckons children to swing, slide and climb below real and artificial trees. The park also includes grassy expanses, barbecue pits, picnic tables and restrooms.

If you want to make sure the kids get to feed ducks (or seagulls, or geese, or coots, or grebes), head to OCEANO LAGOON. The birds here have voracious appetites, which make for some memorable experiences.

Word to the wise: picnicking here's a challenge for even the fastest eaters.

Oceano Dunes State Vehicular Recreation Area
Pier Ave.

(805) 473-7230

www.parks.ca.gov/?page_id=406

$

From Highway 101 take 4th Street south, turn right onto Grand Avenue. Continue straight onto the beach or turn left onto Highway 1/Pacific Boulevard, right onto Pier Avenue, then straight onto the beach.

This 1,500-acre sand playground is popular for off-highway vehicle use, on-beach camping and surf fishing. As the last remaining drive-on beach in California, and one of only a handful on the West Coast, this area can become quite busy with motorists who regularly travel from as far away as Arizona and Nevada. Keep kids close at hand.

The surf is also popular with local longboarders looking to escape the crowds and smaller waves farther north in Pismo Beach. Waves can be larger than up by the pier, but rip tides are also more common here.

Pismo State Beach's Oceano Campground
Pier Ave.

(800) 444-7275

www.slostateparks.com/oceano_campground

$$

From Highway 101 take 4th Street south, turn right onto Grand Avenue, left onto Highway 1/Pacific Boulevard and right onto Pier Avenue.

This 88-site off-beach campground provides a near-beach camping experience for a little less sand in your sandwiches. The campground is also home to the Pismo Nature Center (805-489-8115) which offers hands-on exhibits focused on the natural and cultural history of the area. Docent-led walks are also available. A native plant garden, a trail around Oceano Lagoon, and a trail to the dunes are among the campground's hidden assets.

Oceano Memorial Campground
Pier Avenue

(805) 781-5930

www.slocountyparks.com/activities/oceano.htm

$$

From Highway 101 take 4th Street south, turn right onto Grand Avenue, left onto Highway 1/Pacific Boulevard and right onto Pier Avenue.

A 22-site campground with full hookups ¼-mile from the beach. No reservations accepted; all camping is first come, first served.

OSO FLACO LAKE NATURAL AREA is an ideal family adventure spot.

Chapter 8

Nipomo

Nipomo is a sprawling community spanning Highway 101 about 30 miles south of San Luis Obispo. The community stretches from the curves of old Highway 1 across the wide expanse of the Nipomo Mesa and east to Temetate Ridge. It includes two popular golf courses (Black Lake and Cypress Ridge), a variety of eateries, a handful of shops and is home to thousands of commuters.

The area has long been a horse community, but a boom in development has reduced the accessible riding areas, limited trails access and brought increased traffic that threatens the safety of roadside horseback riders. However, many of the new large developments include public mixed-use pathways popular among horseback riders, walkers, joggers and cyclists.

LETTERS

Nipomo Library
918 West Tefft St.
(805) 929-3994
slolibrary.org
FREE!

From Highway 101 take Tefft Street west, veer left at the Y intersection then turn right into the park.

This branch of the San Luis Obispo City/County Library system offers story time for preschoolers. Call for current hours and schedule.

HISTORY

Dana Adobe
6715 South Oakglen Ave.
(805) 929-5679
danaadobe.org
☛ FREE!-$

From Highway 101 take Tefft Street east and then turn right onto Oakglen Avenue.

La Casa de Dana, the oldest structure in Nipomo, is also California Historical Landmark No. 1033. Construction on this historic home built on a 38,000 acre rancho began in 1839 and was completed in 1851 under the supervision of its owner, designer and chief resident Capt. William G. Dana of Boston, Mass. The famous Yankee sea captain, through his trading with the "Californios," interested the United States in expanding west and annexing California, according to Dana Adobe Nipomo Amigos, the nonprofit corporation organized to rehabilitate and care for the place. The ranch also served as the first stopping place south of San Luis Obispo along El Camino Real. In 1847 it became one of only four designated Pony Express exchange points for the state's first U.S. mail route.

Docent-led tours are generally offered from noon to 4 p.m. Saturdays and Sundays during spring, summer and fall. Winter hours vary. Call for current schedule. Educational group tours are available anytime by reservation.

NATURE

Black Lake Canyon
Guadalupe Road/Zenon Way
(805) 544-9096
www.special-places.org/ecm/Restoration/Black_Lake_Cyn.html
FREE!
From Highway 1 turn east onto Callender Road, turn right onto Sheridan Road, then left onto Laguna Negra Lane and finally left onto Guadalupe Road.

This 140-acre stretch of canyon is home to at least two endangered plant species: marsh sandwort and Gambel's watercress. A well established trail through oaks and eucalyptus is popular with local hikers, joggers and equestrians.

The Land Conservancy of San Luis Obispo County, which preserved the area, continues restoration efforts here. Plans for a trails system and other amenities are in the works.

Monarch Dunes Golf Club
1606 Trilogy Parkway
(805) 343-9459
www.monarchdunesgolf.com
$$$
From Highway 101, turn west onto Tefft Street, right onto Pomeroy and about 3 miles to Willow Road. Turn left onto Willow Road, continue about 2 miles to Via Concha onto which turn left. Continue another mile or so to Trilogy Parkway.

Three courses are planned for this development west of Nipomo. The first course to open was "The Old Course," an 18-hole par-71 course designed to feel like St. Andrew's complete with links-style holes, 35 bunkers and 5 lakes. When completed, the public facility will include an additional 18-hole course and a 9-hole executive course.

Nipomo Community Park
255 Pomeroy Road
(805) 781-5930

www.slocountyparks.com/facilities/communityparks.htm
☞ FREE!

From Highway 101 take Tefft Street west, veer left at the Y intersection then turn right into the park.

This park provides a good stretch for kids of all ages and interests. The park features two play structures (developers were kind enough to leave the good old-fashioned merry-go-round and other older structures in place for visitors enjoyment just a stone's throw from the newfangled structures), restrooms, basketball courts, volleyball courts, baseball fields, soccer fields, equestrian trails, bike paths, undeveloped areas, Nipomo Native Garden and Nipomo Botanical Garden.

Nipomo Creekside Preserve
Behind Olde Towne Plaza
East Tefft St.
(805) 544-9096
FREE!

From Highway 101, take Tefft Street east. Park at Olde Towne Plaza on the left.

This 2 ½ acre preserve located at the confluence of Nipomo Creek and Haystack Creek includes a very short, maintained ring trail with benches made of hay bales and plaster.

OSO FLACO LAKE NATURAL AREA offers toddler- and stroller-friendly walkways.

Oso Flaco Lake Natural Area

West end of Oso Flaco Lake Road off Highway 1

(805) 473-7230

www.dunescenter.org/ottoso.htm

☛ $

Take Highway 1 to Oso Flaco Road. Turn west on Oso Flaco Road which ends at the parking lot.

This natural area offers easy foot access to the dunes (even with stroller). An entrance fee collected by State Parks qualifies visitors to walk the boardwalk over Oso Flaco Lake, through the dunes and out to a vast expanse of sand. Keep an eye out for cormorants drying their wings, ruddy ducks and white pelicans.

Although Oso Flaco Lake is under the general umbrella of Oceano State Vehicular Recreation Area, fees paid to enter the beach by car in Oceano do not translate to pedestrian passage here, or vice versa. Plan to pay separate fees at each gate. Rules here are entirely different, too. No dogs, no horses and no camping are allowed at Oso Flaco, nor are campfires, vehicles, shooting, hunting, bicycling or collecting. Surf fishing, however, is a hit at the beach as are bird watching, kite flying and picnicking.

The non-profit Guadalupe Dunes Center (1055 Guadalupe St., Guadalupe; 805-343-2455) offers educational exhibits, docent-led walks, bird bingo, plant rubbings, scavenger hunts and more throughout the area.

OTHER ADVENTURES

Blacklake Golf Course

1490 Golf Course Lane

(805) 343-1214

www.blacklake.com

$$-$$$

From Highway 101 take Los Berros Road north/west, turn left onto Pomeroy Road, right onto Willow Road, right onto Black Lake Canyon Drive and then left onto Golf Course Lane.

This 27-hole championship course offers three 9-hole layouts including lakes, canyons and ageless oaks, and also offers junior programs.

Eufloria Flowers/Koch Mesa Nursery

885 Mesa Road

(805) 929-4683

www.eufloriaflowers.com

☛ FREE!

From Highway 101 take Tefft Street west. Turn right onto Pomeroy Road, left onto Osage Street and then right onto Mesa Road.

This commercial grower welcomes the public to explore more than eight acres of greenhouses featuring more than 80 varieties of hybrid tea roses grown hydropinically. Guided tours are available by reservation. They offer peeks into the cultivation of long-stem roses that are sold to high-end florists throughout the United States and featured on parade floats during Pasadena's Rose Parade. Educational tours include discussion of Eufloria's practice of using beneficial insects to control pests throughout the greenhouses.

Private tours are available for groups of 15-30 people on the second Tuesday of each month between 8 a.m. and 11 a.m. by appointment; appointments must be made at least one week in advance. Additional tours dates may be possible depending on the season.

The Luffa Farm

1457 Willow Road
(805) 343-0883
www.theluffafarm.biz
☛ FREE!

From Highway 101 take Los Berros Road north/west, turn left onto Pomeroy Road and then right onto Willow Road.

THE LUFFA FARM welcomes visitors of all ages for hands-on tours.

Visitors have been known to show up with fins, snorkels and a variety of other equipment to learn all about luffa, also known as loufa or loufah, that funky "sponge" found in countless showers. This quirky household item has multiple uses, however, and an often unexpected origin. The farm offers tours and, for groups with reservations, tea parties and catered lunches.

Santa Maria Speedway

Hutton Road north of Hwy 166/U.S. 101 interchange
(805) 466-4462
www.santamariaspeedway.com
$-$$

From Highway 101 take the Highway 166 exit and turn west. Turn right onto Hutton Road.

Plenty of noise, flying clay and speed abound at this 1/3-mile oval racetrack every Saturday night from April to mid-October. Stock cars, late model and sprint cars all make regular appearances for points races.

Chapter 9

Los Osos

This growing community just across Morro Bay from the eponymous rock is a great jumping off point for outdoor adventures. The cool, coastal village offers restaurants, shops and outdoor activities that vary from walks in preserved oak woodlands to the community's 17,000-square-foot skate park.

LETTERS

Los Osos Library
2075 Palisades Ave.
(805) 528-1862
www.slolibrary.org/branch.htm
FREE!
From Highway 101 take Los Osos Valley Road west. In Los Osos, turn right onto Palisades Avenue.

Part of the San Luis Obispo County Library system. Story time held Thursdays at 10:30 a.m.

NATURE

Audubon Overlook
End of 4th Street
(805) 528-0540

MONTANA DE ORO STATE PARK offers wonderful views of the north coast, including Morro Bay, Morro Rock and the sandspit that separates the bay from the Pacific Ocean. For a day of true solitude, take a long walk on the spit.

www.morrocoastaudubon.org/sweet.htm
FREE!

From Highway 101 take Los Osos Valley Road west, turn right onto South Bay Boulevard, left onto Santa Ysabel Avenue then right onto Third Street, then turn onto dirt road on right and follow to small parking lot.

This easy-access public viewpoint a short walk from the Baywood Park Pier brings birding to everyone. Bring binoculars, snacks and a camera.

Baywood Park Pier
End of Second Street
(805) 528-6000
FREE!

From Highway 101 take Los Osos Valley Road west, turn right onto South Bay Boulevard, left onto Santa Ysabel Avenue then right onto Second Street.

This short, quiet pier offers exquisite views of the Morro Bay estuary. It's also a good put-in for canoeists and kayakers.

Elfin Forest
North of Santa Ysabel at the end of 11th through 17th Streets
(805) 528-0392
☞ FREE!

THE ELFIN FOREST offers plentiful seating in the shade of ancient oaks.

From Highway 101 take Los Osos Valley Road west, turn right onto South Bay Boulevard, left onto Santa Ysabel, then turn right on any street from 11th to 17th. Wheelchair access at 16th Street.

Few scenic walks with nature in San Luis Obispo County are easier than this one. A 4,000-foot, wheelchair-accessible, wooden boardwalk leads visitors on a loop tour of the 90-acre preserve that features diverse communities of flora and fauna and spectacular views of Morro Bay. Several side trails offer close-up looks at pygmy oaks, wildflowers and the habitat of more than 200 plant species, 110 kinds of birds, 25 species of mammals and 11 species of reptiles and amphibians. Poison oak also grows rampantly throughout the area; be sure you can identify it and keep your eyes peeled.

Volunteers from Small Wilderness Area Preservation (S.W.A.P.) lead walks through the forest the third Saturday of each month. Walks leave promptly at 9:30 a.m.

Los Osos Oaks State Reserve

1 mile south of Los Osos off Los Osos Valley Road
(805) 528-0513 (guided tours: 805-772-2694)
www.parks.ca.gov/default.asp?page_id=597
☛ FREE!

From Highway 101 take Los Osos Valley Road west about 7 miles.

This 85-acre reserve, with its spooky gnarled trees, dappled shade, plentiful bird life and historic past, would be a great place for a child's first hike. Keep children close, however, as poison oak thrives here. The reserve offers easy-to-navigate, dirt trails through ancient sand dunes and groves of centuries-old oak trees.

The trails, which are off limits to bicycles, are not stroller- or wheelchair-friendly. They are not paved and are too narrow, too sandy or too muddy at various points for wheeled vehicles of any sort. The trails pose little challenge for foot traffic. Some fallen trees have been notched to make way for pedestrians. Limbs have been cut off others to clear the way, and bridges have been constructed across spots that apparently are frequently damp or muddy.

Highway noise can drown out the sounds of nature at the outset, but the twisted, thriving old oaks that shelter visitors are captivating. Further into the reserve, the whoosh of passing cars diminishes, leaving visitors to enjoy the sound of rustling leaves and birdsong. About 25 yards past the parking lot, the trail diverges into three paths: one to a Chumash midden, or dump for domestic waste; one to a bluff overlooking Los Osos Creek; and yet another through the grove and on toward the back of the reserve. There are also several well-traveled, though unofficial, trails on which it is easy to roam. Watch for trail signs and wide beaten paths.

According to state parks, the reserve is home to several species of lichen found nowhere else.

Los Osos Community Park
2180 Palisades Ave.

(805) 781-5930

www.slocountyparks.com

FREE!

From Highway 101 take Los Osos Valley Road west, turn right onto Palisades Avenue.

Los Osos Valley School, built in 1872, has been the focal point of this park since the mid 1970s. Today the park also features tennis courts, play structures, restrooms, lawn and a new 17,000-square-foot skate park. A barn and a barbecue area are available by reservation.

Los Osos Skate Park
At Los Osos Community Park

2180 Palisades Ave.

(805) 781-5930

☛ $

From Highway 101 take Los Osos Valley Road west, turn right onto Palisades Avenue.

This brand-new 17,000 square foot concrete skate park features kidney-shaped pool, mini-corner, flat panel, grinding rail, sloped rail, pocket, square bowl, minibowl, extension, waterfall and funbox. Safety rules apply, including mandatory helmet use. Open noon to 5 p.m. Monday through Friday and from 10 a.m. to 5 p.m. weekends.

Monarch Grove
West end of Monarch Lane

FREE!

From Highway 101 take Los Osos Valley Road west, turn right onto Monarch Lane then left onto Inyo Street.

This 18-acre protected grove is home to thousands of over-wintering Monarch butterflies. Trails lead to neighboring state park land and neighborhoods.

Montana de Oro State Park
7 miles south of Los Osos on Pecho Valley Road

General info: (805) 528-0513; docent-led tours (805) 772-7434

www.parks.ca.gov/?page_id=592

☛ FREE!

From Highway 101, take Los Osos Valley Road west and continue through San Luis Obispo, through Los Osos and directly into the park.

For great adventures with nature, head to this 8,000-acre state park off the beaten path. Regulars make it a point to return for the peace of inland valleys, peaks and meadows or the raucous crashing of waves against sand, rock and bluff. The park offers spectacular views, whether visitors are interested in the long sand spit that separates Morro Bay from the ocean, the rugged bluffs further south, the wildflowers of inland valleys, or the sprawling branches of California live oak trees along the slopes. Wildlife also abounds throughout the park, from black-tailed deer to dolphin, coyotes to sea lions, hawks to oystercatchers. The best chance to see inland creatures is during the early morning hours. Take the easy walk along Bluff Trail or head up to one of the peaks.

COON CREEK offers a pleasant family hike with creek crossings, bridges and gnarly oaks.

The only man-made luxuries at Montana de Oro are pit and portable toilets, occasional benches, picnic tables, barbecue stands and an information center. The true luxuries here are the opportunities to spot wildlife, camp between scenic shoreline and rolling hills, commune with nature, draw wildflowers, explore tide pools, and build forts from driftwood.

According to the Natural History Association of San Luis Obispo Coast, the land was used largely for grazing sheep until 1892. Then Alden B. Spooner, Jr., leased, and later purchased, the land around Islay Creek. Among other agricultural uses, he developed a creamery. Goods were transported to and fro via coastal steamers that tied up along the wharf at the southern end of Spooner's Cove.

His northern neighbor, Alexander S. Hazard, also farmed and ran a dairy. It was Hazard who planted hundreds of eucalyptus trees still growing along Pecho Valley Road at the north end of the park. Hazard had hoped to market the long straight lumber as the need for timber increased, but the stringy wood was not suitable for building.

In 1965, the State parks system purchased the land from its last private owner, Irene McAllister.

The wharf, warehouses and many of the agricultural buildings are long gone. Much of the land has returned to its natural state. All that remains of the Hazard and Spooner legacies are the trees, skeletons of the Islay Creek barn and milldam, and the Spooner Ranch House, now used as an information center/museum. A nearby botanical garden names all the species you're likely to see while exploring the park.

Today, typical Montana de Oro views include a red-tail hawk floating on thermals high above Alan Peak, Oats Peak and Valencia Peak, then swooping toward grassland atop the white bluffs. Fifty yards west, a brown pelican glides inches above the Pacific Ocean, watching for fish amongst waves set to crash against jagged Monterey shale and flow into endless tide pools where sea anemone, hermit crabs and sea stars abound.

Most trails are maintained, many remain relatively rugged, with steep climbs and weather-beaten culverts. Favorites for hiking with young children include the Bluff Trail (relatively stroller friendly), Cook Creek Trail (not stroller friendly) and the beach at Spooner's Cove.

The tide pool at Quarry Cove is ideal for watching sea stars and anemones. Islay Creek Road and the Ridge Trail are among local mountain bikers' favorites. The oaks and chaparral up Rattlesnake Flats calls to horseback riders. Hazard Canyon Reef lures surfers to tempt fate in the quest for one excellent ride.

Experienced surfers may be found throughout daylight hours at Hazard Reef, but swimming anywhere along the shore of Montana de Oro is not advisable. The water is fraught with heavy currents, the bottom quickly drops to deep water, and there are no lifeguards on duty.

A brand new, 3-mile bluff-top trail is expected to open at the far northern reaches of the park in late 2006. The trail will extend from the end of Pecho Road (the park's main road) to Crowbar Canyon near Lion Rock. Due to its proximity to Diablo Canyon Nuclear Power Plant, the area may only be available to docent-led tours.

The park's information center, open weekends throughout the year and daily during summer months, offers protection from the cool coastal breeze that blows nearly constantly off the Pacific. Docents at the center can answer questions about park history and wildlife. Park rangers also offer educational nature talks throughout the summer months.

Poison oak flourishes throughout the park. No dogs are allowed on trails, though service dogs are welcome in other areas of the park. Camping is allowed only in designated sites including 50 family campsites off Islay Creek, a handful of primitive hike-in sites and Horse Camp, an area specifically designed to house horses and up to 50 people.

Morro Dunes Natural Preserve
(805) 772-2560

☛ FREE!

Though accessible by boat from Morro Bay, the easiest way to reach this stretch is: from Highway 1 take South Bay Boulevard south, turn left onto Los Osos Valley Road which becomes Pecho Valley Road. Once inside Montana de Oro State Park, turn right onto Sand Spit Road and park, then start walking.

This extension of Montana de Oro State Park stretches 7 miles along the sand spit that protects Morro Bay from the ravages of the sea. This stretch of sand is best for people who are not interested in sharing the beach with others. There are, however, tradeoffs: no services, no restrooms, no lifeguards, dangerous surf, stiff breezes and often fog.

The long spit of sand is little more than a quarter mile across at its widest point. The smooth sandy western side rises quickly into sand dunes that drop drastically on the east side onto the muddy banks of the bay.

With Morro Rock in site and only a quarter mile in width it seems silly to consult a map, but a quick once over will demonstrate how perception of distance changes drastically when there are no buildings, cars, people or trees to offer scale.

This march through soft sand is not an easy one if the end of the spit is the goal, but it's a fantastic place to meander, pick up rocks and ocean detritus, fly a kite or just watch the waves.

Morro Dunes Ecological Reserve – Bayview Unit
South of Highland drive
(707) 944-5500
www.dfg.ca.gov/lands/er/region3/morrodunes.html
FREE!

From Highway 101 take the Los Osos Road exit and head west. Turn left onto Bayview Heights and access the preserve at Calle Cardoniz, or turn right onto Highland Avenue and hop on trailheads south on Palisades, Ravenna or Borderson avenues.

This 237-acre preserve maintained by the U.S. Fish & Wildlife Service is the result of a joint effort of a variety of local organizations including the

SWEET SPRINGS NATURE PRESERVE is the ultimate in hikes for preschool-age children with little or no hiking experience. It's short, includes a variety of habitats, and there are turtles to be spotted in the ponds.

Trust for Public Lands. Eventually, the trust intends to protect a 1,000-acre habitat and trail corridor connecting Morro Bay State Park and Montana de Oro State Park.

For now the reserve includes myriad trails that crisscross the hillside offering fantastic views of the Pacific Ocean, Morro Bay, Morro Rock, and points north. The trails are largely sandy and there are no services. Hikers and horseback riders are welcome. No motorized vehicles are allowed.

Sea Pines Golf Resort

1945 Solano St.

(805) 528-5252

www.seapinesgolfresort.com

$-$$

From Highway 101 take Los Osos Valley Road west, turn right onto Pecho Road, left onto Skyline and continue straight to the resort.

This nine-hole executive golf course also offers a driving range, putting greens, and a chipping area, all with breathtaking views of Morro Bay, the estuary, sand spit, Morro Rock and points beyond.

Sweet Springs Nature Preserve

600 block of Ramona Avenue

(805) 528-0540

www.morrocoastaudubon.org/sweet.htm

FREE!

From Highway 101 take Los Osos Valley Road west, turn right onto South Bay Boulevard, then left onto Ramona Avenue.

This 24-acre preserve offers a very short hike that even the youngest of travelers can manage. Dirt paths are well maintained, and bridges and boardwalks protect vegetation, including tons of poison oak. Turtles are often spotted in the ponds, and plentiful wildlife is there for the viewing along the salt marsh and, ultimately, Morro Bay. Bring binoculars, picnic or snack, jacket and camera.

OTHER ADVENTURES

Orchids of Los Osos

1614 Sage Ave.

(805) 528-0181

www.orchidsoflososos.com

FREE!

From Highway 101 take Los Osos Valley Road west, turn right onto South Bay Boulevard, right onto Nipomo Avenue and then left onto Sage Avenue.

Thousands of delicate orchids grow in five greenhouses that are open by reservation only for group tours. Call ahead, or stop by the associated greenhouse which is open to the public.

BLACK HILL affords a relatively easy hike up one of the smaller volcanic peaks in San Luis Obispo County.

Chapter 10

Morro Bay

The city by the bay is nearly as entertaining as the bay itself. Activities include dining, shopping, playing in numerous parks, feeding seals at the aquarium, watching wildlife in the bay, whale watching, playing chess on the giant chess board, sport fishing, kayaking, biking, skating, kite flying, underwater tours, dinner cruises, brunch cruises, exploring the estuary, golfing, miniature golfing, camping, surfing and simply relaxing on the long, sandy beach.

Expect morning and afternoon fog which often remains thick throughout the day in the hottest summer months. Also expect cold water and be prepared for unpredictable currents at all area beaches.

Morro Bay Recreation and Parks Department manages and maintains several parks that cater to families with children. All are free to the public for typical day use, but permits are required for special events.

ARTS

Morro Bay Art Association Gallery
835 Main Street
(805) 772-2504
www.morrobayartassociation.org
FREE!
From Highway 1 take Morro Bay Boulevard west, and then turn right onto Main Street.
This small gallery features works by local artists.

The Bay Theater
464 Morro Bay Blvd.
(805) 772-2444
$$
From Highway 1 take Morro Bay Boulevard west.
A one-screen movie theater featuring Hollywood blockbusters.

LETTERS

Morro Bay Public Library
625 Harbor Street
(805) 772-6394
FREE!

From Highway 1 take Morro Bay Boulevard west, then veer right onto Harbor Street.

Preschool story time weekly. Call for current schedule.

NATURE

Anchor Memorial Park

Embarcadero at west end of Dunes Street

(805) 772-6278

FREE!

From Highway 1 take Morro Bay Boulevard west, turn right onto Main Street, left onto Harbor Street, right onto Embarcadero, then left onto Dunes Street.

This tiny park, also referred to as Dunes Street Park, offers access to fishing and picnic benches.

Azure Street Coastal Access

FREE!

From Highway 1 turn left onto San Jacinto Street, left onto Sandalwood Avenue and right onto Azure Street to the parking lot at its end.

A small parking lot at the end of the street provides parking for those willing to take an easy walk through the dunes to the Morro Strand State Beach/Atascadero Beach. This is also the northern access to Cloisters Open Space and restrooms are available here.

Bayshore Bluffs Park

Bayshore Drive

(805) 772-6278

FREE!

From Highway 1 take Morro Bay Boulevard west, turn left onto Main Street, then right onto Sandpiper Lane (through Bayshores Village development).

This quiet, little-known patch of grass offers picnic tables, individual barbecues, restrooms, benches and fantastic bay views. Walk along the paved pathway under the arched cypress to find stairs that lead to the shore.

Beachcomber Drive Coastal Access

FREE!

From Highway 1 turn left onto San Jacinto Street, right onto Sandalwood Avenue, jog left onto Sienna Street and right onto Beachcomber Drive.

Watch for signs indicating public walkways between beachfront homes to less-crowded stretches of Morro Strand State Beach.

Centennial Parkway

Embarcadero Road & Front Street

(805) 772-6278

☛ FREE!

From Highway 1 take Morro Bay Boulevard west, turn right onto Main Street, left onto Harbor Street then left onto Front Street.

This tiny park across the street from the public restrooms features the city's Giant Chess Board. The 16-foot square concrete board is available for play. Call weekdays to reserve the 18-20 pound chess pieces.

The park also includes picnic tables, benches and a restroom across the street.

Cerro Cabrillo Area
Access from South Bay Boulevard or Turri Road
(805) 772-2560
www.parks.ca.gov
☛ FREE!

From Highway 1 take South Bay Boulevard South. Two turn offs on the east side of the road mark the trailheads.

This extension of Morro Bay State Park encompasses acres of native plants, Cerro Cabrillo, Tiki Head and miles of trails accessible to hikers and mountain bikers alike. The eight mapped trails include Park Ridge, Live Oak, Portola View Point (elev. 329 feet), Quarry, Canet, Crespi, Chumash, Chorro and Cerro Cabrillo (elev. 911 feet). The area is aflutter with birds including a plethora of raptors who no doubt feast on the bountiful rabbits. Coyotes are also regularly seen here and the area is known to be a mountain lion habitat, though they have seldom been seen.

The Park Ridge Trail offers the easiest walk for young hikers or cyclists with some off-pavement experience. Quarry Trail offers more elevation change, but remains moderately strenuous as it leads away from the noise of the city, past the long-since-abandoned quarries below an aptly named rock formation known as Tiki Head and eventually to the park boundary fence. Live Oak Trail provides access to the trail that climbs to Portola Viewpoint.

Among the most diverse trails in the park is Crespi Trail. The single-track trail named for Father Juan Crespi who passed through the area in 1769 rises and falls with the contours of Cerro Hutash before dropping into an oak grove. Older children with plenty of off-pavement experience may enjoy this route.

Cloisters Park
Coral Avenue
(805) 772-6278
☛ FREE!

From Highway 1 take San Jacinto Street west, turn left onto Coral Avenue
Expansive park includes play structures, group and individual barbecue areas, restrooms, walking trails and beach boardwalks. Open turf areas give way to protected dunes through which paved trails dotted with interpretive signs lead to the beach.

Coleman Park
Coleman Road
(805) 772-6278
FREE!

From Highway 1 take Morro Bay Boulevard west, turn right onto Main Street, left onto Beach Street, right onto Embarcadero which becomes Coleman Drive and follow it to its end.

A timeless park that provides beach access, swings, picnic tables, restrooms and benches adjacent to the dunes and just a stone's throw from Morro Rock. It is also home to a fenced-in, above-ground skate park run by the city. Rollerblades are allowed in the skate park, but no bicycles or scooters.

Del Mar Park
Ironwood Avenue
(805) 772-6278
FREE!

From Highway 1 turn east onto San Jacinto Street, then left onto Ironwood Avenue.

This evolving park has been home to a BMX track and roller hockey rink in its day. Lasting features include play structures, picnic tables, restrooms, barbecues, basketball and volleyball courts, trails, benches, a horseshoe pit and loads of grass.

Heron Rookery Preserve
(805) 772-2560
FREE!

From Highway 1 exit Morro Bay Boulevard and turn west. Turn left onto Kern Avenue which becomes State Park Road.

Eucalyptus and cypress trees provide roosting and nesting sites for cormorants, egrets and herons. Visitors can view lively brooding behavior in the spring.

Lila H. Keiser Park
Park Street/Atascadero Road
(805) 772-6278
FREE!

From Highway 1 take the Atascadero Road/Highway 41 exit, then turn west onto Atascadero Road and left onto Park Street.

This sports park behind the city's three famous stacks includes baseball and softball diamonds, soccer fields, horseshoe pit, picnic tables, individual and group barbecue areas, a restroom, play structures and benches.

Mariner Park
Embarcadero Road
(805) 772-6278
www.morro-bay.ca.us
FREE!

From Highway 1 take Morro Bay Boulevard west, turn right onto Main Street, left onto Harbor Street then left onto Embarcadero.

This tiny park serves to provide public access to the bay and its fishing opportunities. The park also has benches and picnic tables.

Monte Young Park
South Street/Shasta
(805) 772-6278
FREE!

From Highway 1 take Morro Bay Boulevard west and then turn left onto Shasta Avenue.

This neighborhood park includes tennis courts, play structure, restroom and picnic benches.

Morro Bay City Park
Morro Bay Blvd/Harbor St.
(805) 772-6278
FREE!

From Highway 1 take Morro Bay Boulevard west.

This is a triangular park bordered on two sides by busy streets, but there's room to run kids on the grass or play a pickup game of basketball or shuffleboard. Also includes picnic tables, individual and group barbecue areas, play structure and restroom.

Morro Bay Golf Course
State Park Road
(805) 782-8060
$$-$$$

From Highway 1 exit Morro Bay Boulevard and turn west. Turn left onto Kern Avenue which becomes State Park Road.

This 18-hole course located within Morro Bay State Park offers junior rates, lessons, pro shop and driving range all overlooking the scenic bay.

Morro Bay State Park
(805) 772-2560
www.parks.ca.gov/?page_id=594
FREE!

From Highway 1 exit Morro Bay Boulevard and turn west. Turn left onto Kern Avenue which becomes State Park Road.

This 2,700-acre park features trails, marina, boat launch and boat rentals, camping, an 18-hole golf course and other amenities.

A relatively short and easy walk to the top of Black Hill east of the golf course affords expansive views of the coastline from Montana de Oro to San Simeon and well inland. There are no services at the trailhead, so use the restroom elsewhere and pack water, lunch, binoculars and a camera.

The park's marina offers a café, human-powered boat rentals and views. It's a fun place to watch little sail boats come and go.

Morro Estuary National Preserve

Can be viewed from Morro Bay State Park Marina or Sweet Springs Nature Preserve in Los Osos

(805) 772-3834

FREE!

From Highway 1 exit Morro Bay Boulevard and turn west. Turn left onto Kern Avenue which becomes State Park Road and leads past the marina.

This highly protected 800-acre salt marsh located within Morro Bay State Park is generally available only for observation from afar. Bring binoculars and lunch to enjoy myriad waterfowl and shorebirds living throughout the tidal slough.

Morro Rock Nature Preserve

Coleman Drive

☛ FREE!

From Highway 1 take Morro Bay Boulevard west, turn right onto Main Street, left onto Beach Street, right onto Embarcadero which becomes Coleman Drive and follow it to its end.

Most visitors eventually find their way to Morro Rock, the city's 576-foot-tall landmark and namesake. The gigantic 20-million-year-old outcropping juts from the ocean at the mouth of the bay. It's one in a chain of nine lava plugs that extend east past San Luis Obispo. While others are popular among hikers (like Bishop Peak in San Luis Obispo), no climbing or hiking is allowed on Morro Rock. It's dangerous, and it's also a nesting place for the rare peregrine falcon.

Waves and dangerous currents once protected the rock, sometimes referred to as "The Gibraltar of the Pacific," from all sides. According to various local historians, early written references to the landmark date back to 1542 when explorer Juan Cabrillo took note of it.

Today, California State Historic Landmark No. 821 is accessible by car, bicycle or on foot via the World War II era causeway at the end of Embarcadero. Visitors often sport binoculars in hopes of catching a glimpse of the endangered peregrine falcons that nest high in the crags, and the otters that raft in the ocean eddies below.

The jetty offers protection from wind and surf along the beach north of the road. It's a good place to look for shells and rocks at low tide, but the current can be strong here.

The beach on the north side of the rock offers epic surfing for the experienced. Summer waves are typically small, but winter boomers combined with the rip tide alongside the rock make this a winter spot for experts.

Morro Strand State Beach/Atascadero Beach

(805) 772-2560

www.parks.ca.gov/

☞ FREE!

From Highway 1 turn west onto Atascadero Road to reach the most southerly stretch of this beach. See also Studio Drive Coastal Access, Azure Street Coastal Access, Beachcomber Drive Coastal Access, and Morro Strand State Beach/Atascadero Beach.

Morro Strand State Beach is divided into two sections. The southern section, sometimes referred to as Atascadero Beach, stretches from Atascadero Road north to Yerba Buena Street. The northerly stretch of sand runs from 24th Street in Cayucos to south of Chaney Avenue. There are, however, no lines in the sand for the entire section of sandy beach that stretches from Morro Rock to the bluffs north of Cayucos Pier.

The area is known for its fairly gentle waves and views of Morro Rock. A fairly steady ocean breeze makes this and northern neighbor Morro Strand State Beach popular among kite enthusiasts, windsurfers, kite-skiers and kite-surfers. Local surfers come here when it's too crowded at Morro Rock or in fall and winter months when the waves here hollow out.

At low tide it is possible to walk via this beach from Morro Rock to the bluffs north of Cayucos Pier. The three-mile stretch of beach between 24th Street in Cayucos and Yerba Buena in Morro Bay is particularly popular for

A surfboard glistens on shore. At low tide it's possible to walk from Morro Rock to Cayucos.

wind sports: kite sailing, kiting, and windsurfing. But it isn't always windy. Swimming and surfing are also favorites along this long sandy stretch.

Expect morning and afternoon fog which often stretches clear through the day in the hottest summer months. Also expect cold water and be prepared for unpredictable currents at all area beaches.

Museum of Natural History

Morro Bay State Park
State Park Road
(805) 772-2694
www.MorroBayMuseum.org
☛ FREE!-$

From Highway 1 exit Morro Bay Boulevard and turn west. Turn left onto Kern Avenue which becomes State Park Road.

One of the most beautiful views of Morro Bay is hidden behind a great big rock. Not Morro Rock, but a miniature morro that conceals this museum from the park's main thoroughfare. The museum, opposite the campground and down the road from the golf course, is an underutilized treasure along the bay.

The museum itself is quite small, but a 2002 renovation greatly improved the collection and presentation. More than 25 displays, many of them hands-

The MUSEUM OF NATURAL HISTORY has one of the best bay views available.

on, emphasize local fish, birds, Chumash people indigenous to the Central Coast, and local geology.

What the museum lacks in quantity it makes up for in quality, staff and special programs. Every weekend, there are puppet shows, story hours, kids' cinema and special hands-on activities for children as well as docent-led walks.

Open 10 a.m. to 5 p.m. most days. Call ahead for current schedule.

North Point Natural Area
Toro Lane
(805) 772-6278
FREE!

From Highway 1 turn west onto Yerba Buena Street then immediately right onto Toro Lane.

As its title suggests, this area has not been covered in turf but left in its natural state. A bluff-top trail provides a quick retreat from civilization and offers ocean views and beach access.

Studio Drive Coastal Access
FREE!

From Highway 1 turn west onto Studio Drive.

Public access to Morro Strand State Beach is available on marked pathways between homes near cross streets of Rapf, Mayer, Thalberg, Del Mar, El Sereno, Gracia and Juanita avenues. Parking is extremely limited, but the area is prime for long walks and good surf.

Tidelands Park
South end of Embarcadero
(805) 772-6278
☛ FREE!

From Highway 1 take Morro Bay Boulevard west, turn left onto Main Street, right onto Beach Street, right onto Pacific Street and left onto Embarcadero.

Children at heart are invited to play roles on a wooden ship in the park's sea of sand overlooking the bay. The nearby boat launch provides added interest. Facilities include restrooms, picnic tables, and individual and group barbecue areas.

OTHER ADVENTURES

Baron's Orchids
465 Harbor St.
(805) 772-1320
www.baronsorchids.com
FREE!

From Highway 1 take Morro Bay Boulevard west, then veer right onto Harbor Street.

This commercial orchid grower allows public access to its greenhouses during normal operating hours (open daily). Call ahead for group tours or if you'd like a staff member to guide.

The Embarcadero

Embarcadero from Tidelands Park to Front Street

(805) 772-4467

FREE!

From Highway 1 take Morro Bay Boulevard west, turn right onto Main Street, left onto Beach Street and continue to Embarcadero.

THE EMBARCADERO offers parks, shopping, views and public docks.

Though the Embarcadero has its fair share of shops featuring postcards, T-shirts and other memorabilia, the percentage of art studios and specialty stores is on the rise. It is also home to kite shops, restaurants, boat charter companies, a mom-n-pop aquarium, nature center and Tidelands Park, a great place for kids to run.

Morro Bay Aquarium

595 Embarcadero

(805) 772-7647

www.morrobay.com/ morrobayaquarium/

$

From Highway 1 take Morro Bay Boulevard west, turn left onto Main Street, right onto Beach Street, right onto Pacific Street and left onto Embarcadero.

Though not expansive or particularly time consuming, this small 40-year-old aquarium includes little tanks of sea life specimens as well as pools filled with vociferous seals and sea lions. For a small fee, visitors can feed the animals rehabilitating here after being found sick, injured or abandoned.

Morro Bay Estuary Nature Center

601 Embarcadero, Suite 11 (upstairs)

(805) 772-3834

www.morrocoastaudubon.org/mbnep.htm
FREE!

From Highway 1 take Morro Bay Boulevard west, turn left onto Main Street, right onto Beach Street, right onto Pacific Street and left onto Embarcadero.

The center strives to educate the public about the past, present and potential future of the Morro Bay Estuary. Exhibits offer insights into the estuary and watershed. Hands-on displays offer tips for identifying local birds and other wildlife. The center also provides docent-led workshops for school groups with advance reservations.

Morro Fleece Works
1920 Main Street
(805) 772-9665
FREE!

From Highway 1 take Main Street east.

This specialty business scours, picks, cards and roves wool from llama, alpaca and other wool-bearing animals. Batts and felt sheets are also made here. Tours are available by appointment only. Groups preferred.

Chapter 11

Cayucos

This tiny, sunny, funky beach town on Highway 1 between Morro Bay and Cambria is an ideal place to beach with kids. The wide, flat sands are only steps away from ice cream parlors and taquerias - a blessing for anyone with hungry children (or hungry adults). Southern exposure means Cayucos is likely to see fog burn off earlier than Morro Bay - another important consideration in choosing beaches.

The charm of Cayucos is that it hasn't changed in years. The population remains 3,000. Old homes just keep getting better. Old shops continue to provide good food and entertainment. And the beach retains its beauty.

Everything in Cayucos is within walking distance.

ARTS

Cayucos Art Association Gallery
10 Cayucos Drive

CAYUCOS PIER offers benches, birds and beautiful views.

(805) 995-2049

www.cayucos.org/caa

FREE!

From Highway 1 take the Cayucos Drive exit and continue west to the end of the street.

Local artist show their works in this pierside gallery that rotates its exhibits every six weeks. Paintings, photographs, sculptures and crafts are all included. There are also bins of artwork, cards and crafts for sale. Open Tuesdays through Sundays from 1 p.m. to 4 p.m.

Cayucos Mural Walk

Various locations

(805) 995-3539

www.cayucos.org/muralsociety

FREE!

Take some time to walk the city's path of mural art for a different view of this seaside community. Grab a map off the Cayucos Mural Society's website (listed here), or simply begin walking up Ocean Avenue from 3rd Street, turn right onto Cayucos Drive, left onto Birch Avenue and wrap up the tour at Hardie Park Pool on B Street.

LETTERS

Cayucos Library

248 S. Ocean Avenue

(805) 995-3312

FREE!

From Highway 1 take Cayucos Drive west, and then turn left onto Ocean Avenue.

Part of the San Luis Obispo County Library system. Preschool story time offered Wednesdays at 11 a.m.

NATURE

Cayucos Pier

West end of Cayucos Drive

(805) 781-5930

www.slostateparks.com/cayucos_state_beach/

☛ FREE!

From Highway 1 take the Cayucos Drive exit and continue west to the end of the street.

The 125-year-old Cayucos Pier is a popular spot for pedestrians and fishermen alike. Benches along both sides of the gently swaying pier offer visitors picturesque views of sand, surf and seagulls. Below, body boarders and surfers wait for the next big wave.

Cayucos Skate Park

Norma Rose Park

(805) 995-2401

FREE!

From Highway 1 take 13th Street east, turn immediately right onto Cabrillo Avenue.

A 10,000-square-foot concrete skate park is in the works at Norma Rose Park and may be completed by the time you peruse this page. Meanwhile, head to the Veterans' Hall (10 Cayucos Drive) where a 5,400-square-foot, well-used, lighted park is free for all who wear helmets. Until the new park opens, this one will provide skate freedom daily from dawn to 8 p.m.

Cayucos State Beach

West end of Cayucos Drive

(805) 781-5930

www.slostateparks.com/cayucos_state_beach/

☛ FREE!

From Highway 1 take the Cayucos Drive exit and continue west to the end of the street.

The 10-mile stretch of sand that begins in Morro Bay includes great climbing rocks midbeach, then turns to tide pools at its northern end. On shore, driftwood serves as the medium for artists and architects. At the hand of visitors, it becomes shade structures for parents, teepees for children or stickpeople who occupy sandcastles.

CAYUCOS STATE BEACH seems to stretch on forever.

A good collection of playground equipment near the pier includes full-size slides, swings, jungle gyms and a smaller toddler set. Restrooms and public showers are at the base of the pier, and kayak and surfboard rentals are available nearby.

Though the most obvious access to the beach is downtown at the pier, there are a number of marked public access pathways between homes along Pacific Avenue near 12th, 9th, 3rd and 1st streets. Head down the steep 24th Street stairs to hit a hot surfing spot, sometimes called Studios.

Coastal Viewpoint
290 Pacific Avenue
FREE!
From Highway 1 take 13th Street exit, turn west onto 13th Street, then right onto Pacific Avenue
This public viewpoint offers expansive views of Estero Bay and its miles of sandy beaches and coastal bluffs.

Estero Bluffs
West of Highway 1 from North Ocean Street to Villa Creek
(805) 772-7434
www.slostateparks.com/estero_bluffs/
☛ FREE!
Very large dirt pullouts along the coastal side of the highway mark this relatively little known 355-acre public open space. Some highlights of this California State Parks property include incredibly serene coves, seals, sea lions, otters, driftwood, tide pools, herons, egrets and 9 miles of trails along bluffs.

The beach at Villa Creek typically is loaded with driftwood ideal for a day of creating with kids. The same beach is ideal habitat for snowy plover, so some sections of the park are fenced off during nesting season.

The largest parking area is north of Cayucos along Highway 1, but the bluffs can also be accessed legally from the north end of North Ocean Avenue.

Hardie Park
B Street & Birch Avenue
FREE!
From Highway 1 take the Cayucos Drive exit, head west, then turn right onto Birch Avenue.
This grassy park has plentiful swings, play structures for big kids and a fenced in play structure area for smaller ones. There's also a large covered picnic area, barbecue, tennis courts and a restroom.

For driftwood and other beach oddities, head to the north side of Cayucos Pier.

Hardie Park Pool
Birch Avenue and "B" Street
www.slocountyparks.com/facilities/pools.htm
$

From Highway 1 take the Cayucos Drive exit, head west, turn right onto Birch Avenue and then left onto "B" Street.

This community pool maintained and run by county parks is across the street from Hardie Park. It's open Memorial Day to Labor Day.

Norma Rose Park
Cabrillo Avenue
(805) 995-2401
FREE!

From Highway 1 take 13th Street east, turn immediately right onto Cabrillo Avenue.

Locals have big plans for this park wedged between the east side of Highway 1 and the Cayucos Cemetery. Amenities will include turf, paths, basketball courts, picnic areas, an off-leash dog park, restrooms and a 10,000-square-foot cement skate park complete with pool and other obstacles.

Old Creek Road
FREE!

From Highway 1 turn east onto Old Creek Road.

This scenic drive past Whale Rock Reservoir also serves as a great ride for experienced road cyclists. It's particularly attractive when the wildflowers are out (late spring), as the hills turn golden (early summer) and when the colors change (late fall). While the area is also beautiful in mid-summer, heat makes it a killer ride that is best delayed until cooler weather prevails.

The rural road meanders along Willow Creek before heading up and past the reservoir, then on to the ridge and eventually across Highway 46. Here the road changes names to Santa Rosa Creek Road. The route also turns somewhat treacherous here. The steep, rough pavement has proven tough to maintain, so riders must watch for swells, dips and extreme cracks.

The lower portion of the road offers a relatively easy, peaceful and seldom-traveled road to Main Street in Cambria.

Santa Rita Road
FREE!
From Highway 1 turn east onto Old Creek Road, then right onto Santa Rita Road.

This mountain bike ride offers spectacular views in a low-traffic area. Begin at the intersection of Old Creek Road and Santa Rita Road. The lower portion along Old Creek offers family friendly riding, but the road turns to more than 3 miles of dirt and a long, steady climb will weed out most of the little ones. Experienced riders, teens and their energetic chaperones who want to continue east from here will be rewarded with expansive views from the ridge.

From the ridge, continue east to Vineyard Road and on to Templeton, or blast back west to the car.

Sea West Ranch
West of Highway 1 near Harmony
(805) 772-7434
FREE!
This 746-acre state parks property remained closed to public access in early 2006 and no opening date had been scheduled. The park's plan, however, includes development of 7 miles of hiking trails, picnic areas and a wetland loop trail with access to a rustic caretaker's cabin.

Whale Rock Reservoir
Old Creek Road
(805) 995-3701
www.slocity.org/utilities/sources.asp#Whale
$
From Highway 1, turn east onto Old Creek Road.

This reservoir was built in 1961 to serve as a water source for San Luis Obispo. The result: a scenic reservoir surrounded by serene landscape and offering breathtaking views of the Pacific Ocean. It's an inexpensive spot, but there are plenty of restrictions: no body contact with the reservoir water, no boats, no live bait, dogs must be on leash.

The 2 miles of shoreline trail is actually an old dirt road that is open to bicyclists and hikers from 7 a.m. to 4 p.m. Wednesdays through Sundays beginning the last weekend in April and running through Nov. 15. There is no winter access.

Shoreline fishing is allowed with a California fishing license. Regular piscine sightings include steelhead trout, western sucker, catfish and blue gill. Facilities also include picnic tables at each end of the trail, outhouses and garbage cans.

OTHER ADVENTURES

The Abalone Farm

Highway 1

(805) 995-2495

www.abalonefarm.com

FREE!

Call for directions.

This 38-year-old business venture has one of the most spectacular views of Estero Bay from its bluff-top location hidden behind rolling hills west of Highway 1. The largest and oldest producer of California red abalone in the U.S. opens its doors by reservation only for group educational tours from May to September. Visitors meander from one outdoor tank to another while a guide explains the history of the business and the system that provides fresh seawater for the marine snails that can grow up to 12 inches across and fetch more than $100 per pound.

Cotton Tail Creek Ranch

2005 Cottontail Creek Road

(805) 995-1787

Cottontailcreek.com

$$$+

From Highway 1 take Old Creek Road east past Whale Rock Reservoir. Turn left onto Cottontail Creek Road.

Pricey accommodations may be affordable for a handful of families, but the amenities may be worth it. Rural setting at this ranch guesthouse that welcomes, even encourages, visitors to bring their hiking boots, mountain bikes and horses.

A ceramics studio in the barn is the source of many works on display in the ranch house. Special services can also be provided upon request for an additional fee.

Chapter 12

Cambria

Cambria, a traditionally artsy community both exposed to the ravages of the Pacific Coast and nestled in the wooded rolling coastal hills, is a community divided by Highway 1. The western portion offers supreme ocean views, coastal access and hikes. The eastern portion offers shops, restaurants, parks and historic points of interest.

The beaches here are, largely, fantastic places to hunt for the perfect rock. That was Grandma Ruth Poore's favorite part. "The rocky beaches have this special sound when the tide rolls out from the rocks," she said. "I love that sound."

ARTS

Pewter Plough Playhouse
824 Main St.
(805) 927-3877
www.pewterploughplayhouse.org

CAMBRIA PINES LODGE is among Cambria businesses that welcome garden tourists.

$$$

From Highway 1 turn east onto Main Street.

For nearly three decades community players have gathered on stage here to present their best with six productions each year. A monthly readers' theater is free and open to the general public. (It also seeks readers regularly.) Call or check online for current schedule.

Allied Arts Association Schoolhouse Gallery

880 Main St.

(805) 927-8190

www.artistsofcambria.com

FREE!

From Highway 1 turn east onto Main Street.

Local artists show their works throughout the year in the historic Santa Rosa Schoolhouse. Exhibits include a variety of media and moods. The association also sponsors several public events throughout the year including a Home Tour, Spring Music Competition, Pinedorado Art Show and Reception and the Petals and Palettes Garden and Art Show. The association also includes a theater arts group.

LETTERS

Cambria Library

900 Main Street

(805) 927-4336

www.slolibrary.org

FREE!

From Highway 1 turn east onto Main Street.

Part of the San Luis Obispo County Library system. Preschool storytime offered every Thursday at 10:15 a.m.

NATURE

Cambria area coves

FREE!

From Highway 1 turn west on Ardath Drive. Turn right onto Randall Drive, then left onto Lampton Street, then right onto Sherwood Drive.

Like other coastal communities, Cambria offers public access to beaches even in private neighborhoods. Watch for marked pathways between homes along Sherwood Drive near its intersections with Harvey and Drake streets.

Cambria Coastal Viewpoint

Harvey/Sherwood Dr.

From Highway 1, turn west on Ardath Drive. Turn right onto Randall Drive, then left onto Lampton Street, then right onto Sherwood Drive.

A ice place for a quick stop or a long break with fantastic Pacific views.

Cambria Community Park
Rodeo Grounds Road
(805) 927-6223
www.cambriacsd.org
FREE!

From Highway 1 take Main Street east, turn right onto Burton Drive, then right onto Rodeo Grounds Road.

This proposed 17½-acre park on a portion of East-West Ranch is still in the works, but it may eventually include a community center and athletic fields, among other amenities. Call for current status.

Cambria Dog Park
(805) 927-7229
FREE!

From Highway 1 turn east onto Main Street. The park is near the intersection of Main Street and Santa Rosa Creek Road.

Local dog walkers have personalized this small fenced park at the edge of town. A shade structure, benches, chairs and tables offer respite for weary dog owners while their canine companions roam free, take a drink, share a dog toy and sniff to their little hearts' content. It's run by volunteers, so feel free to pick up a rake or shovel and pitch in, or to adopt the park for a family, club or Scout project.

Cambria Pines Lodge Organic Herb and Produce Gardens
2905 Burton Drive
(800) 445-6868
www.cambriapineslodge.com/garden.htm
FREE!

From Highway 1 take Main Street east to Burton Drive.

This privately-owned lodge welcomes visitors onto its 25 acres of gardens including a manicured herb garden and a certified organic vegetable garden that supplies the property's restaurant.

East-West Ranch
Windsor Drive
(805) 927-6223
www.cambriacsd.org
☞ FREE!

From Highway 1 take either Windsor Drive west to its terminus at the north edge of the open space or turn west on Ardath Drive. From Ardath, turn right onto Madison, left onto Orland Drive, then right onto South Windsor Drive which terminates at the south end of the open space.

Coastal bluffs and pine forests are among the highlights of EAST-WEST RANCH.

This 417-acre open space that divides the northern and southern coastal neighborhoods offers neighbors and visitors a peaceful escape from the developed world. There are literally a dozen trails that crisscross the property.

Among the most family friendly is a 1-mile trail along the bluff-top marine terrace that offers easy walks for families with views as far north as Piedras Blancas Light Station, beyond crashing waves to the horizon, or inland to tree-covered rolling hills. For added difficulty, and a different perspective, take the 4,400-foot spur along the creek where observant hikers may notice stream bank stabilization efforts including built-in trout habitat devices.

The area is popular for hikers, joggers and dog walkers. Bicycles are allowed on designated trails only.

Take binoculars and have a seat on any of the benches along the route. A quick peek and you're likely to see otters, seals, sea lions and, in season, whales. Spend more time on the property, especially in the early morning hours, and you may see deer, bobcats, skunks, raccoons or even red-legged frogs.

Initially access was limited and only the bluff trail was open for exploration, but plans continue toward development of other areas of the ranch. They include five stands of Monterey pine covering 65 acres, additional stands of coastal live oak, seabluff scrub, grassland, wetlands, marshes and coastal scrub.

Open dawn to dusk. Watch out for the bone-chilling coastal breeze. Bring a windbreaker.

Lampton Cliffs Park

At the intersection of South Windsor Boulevard and Lampton Street
(805) 781-5930
www.slocountyparks.com

FREE!

From Highway 1 turn west onto Ardath Drive. Turn right onto Randall Drive, then left onto Lampton Street and continue west to the park.

For a seriously out-of-the-way rocky escape, seek out this tiny beach bound by coastal bluffs with nothing but rough seas, jagged rock tidepools and nearly guaranteed privacy. This 2.2-acre park has gone through multiple renovations thanks to the waves that pound the cliffs here. The latest incarnation includes a well-maintained loop trail atop the bluff and stairs to a rocky beach below. The beach is only accessible at low tide, so check your tide table before heading out if beach access is critical to your visit.

Lawn Bowling

Joslyn Center

950 Main Street

(805) 927-3364

$$

From Highway 1 turn east onto Main Street.

Lawn bowling is coming back into vogue. The Joslyn Center, generally a center for those 18 and older, now offers a lawn bowling mentoring program for youngsters. Adult members (membership is $20 per year) are welcome to bring along younger bowlers for weekend games.

Linn's Original Farm Store

6275 Santa Rosa Creek Road

(805) 927-1499

www.linnsfruitbin.com

FREE!

From Highway 1 turn east onto Main Street, then east onto Santa Rosa Creek Road. Continue several miles along this paved, narrow, country road lined with oak and sycamore trees.

The farm store that kicked off the Linns' restaurant experiment continues to offer the same great pies, jams and other goods it has since 1977. But kids will be most interested in the grassy spot under an ancient sycamore next to an inviting creek.

The Linns welcome families to picnic here.

McCall Farm

6520 Santa Rosa Creek Road

(805) 927-3140

www.mccallfarm.com/harvest.html

$-$$$

From Highway 1 turn east onto Main Street. At Santa Rosa Creek Road turn east and continue 5 miles to the farm.

This farm offers pick-your-own apples, tomatoes and peppers in season roughtly September to November. The farm also offers bed and breakfast.

Moonstone Beach
Moonstone Beach Drive
☞ FREE!

From Highway 1 turn west onto Windsor Boulevard then immediately right onto Moonstone Beach Drive. Moonstone beach extends from Chatham Lane north about ¼ mile.

The beach is named for its rough sand – or shall we say smooth rock – and is known best for its tide pools, bluff-top boardwalk and frequent visits from seals, otters and local surfers. My grandmother, Ruth Poore, always loved this beach for the treasures hidden among the teeny tiny rocks. "Sometimes you can find some that look like jade, sometimes those that are white like moonstones. To me it is a treasure," she said.

While surfers enjoy the swell at the southern end of Moonstone Beach, the currents along this stretch of the North Coast are hazardous for swimmers, young waders and pets.

The boardwalk is wide enough for strollers and wheelchairs. Bring binoculars for closer views of seals, otters and surfers. There are restrooms at the southern end of the beach.

Santa Rosa Creek Road
FREE!

From Highway 1 turn east onto Main Street the continue east onto Santa Rosa Creek Road.

This rural road that leads from Cambria to Highway 46 offers a scenic setting for motorists and experienced cyclists alike. This road less traveled is particularly scenic for wildflower tours (late spring) and autumn colors.

The road that takes off east from Main Street offers a relatively easy ride, but it's narrow, so only recommended for more experienced cyclists. Santa Rosa Creek Road begins a steady climb that turns into an outright challenge toward the top complete with rough pavement, swells, dips and cracks.

Across Highway 46 the road is called Old Creek Road. Enjoy spectacular views from the ridges before plummeting back down toward Willow Creek, Whale Rock Reservoir and eventually Cayucos.

Shamel Park
5455 Windsor Blvd.
www.slocountyparks.com
FREE!

From Highway 1 turn west onto Windsor Boulevard.

This 6-acre county park is bordered on the west by the Pacific Ocean and on the northeast by Santa Rosa Creek. The park offers beautiful ocean and inland views, lawn, playground, horseshoe pits, barbecue, restrooms, and public swimming pool.

Shamel Park Pool
5455 Windsor Blvd.
www.slocountyparks.com/facilities/pools.htm
$
From Highway 1 turn west onto Windsor Boulevard.
This county-operated pool offers public swimming from Memorial Day
Weekend to Labor Day. Call ahead for hours.

Skate Park
1000 Main Street
(805) 927-7776
FREE!
From Highway 1 turn east onto Main Street.
Helmets are required for skaters of all ages at this free park. Riders 12
and under must also wear pads. From 10 a.m. to dusk, riders are invited to
enjoy the features that include a 50-foot-by-100-foot half pipe and a
pyramid.

OTHER ADVENTURES

Covell's Pines by the Sea Ranch
5694 Bridge St.
(805) 927-3398
$$$
From Highway 1 turn east onto Main Street, then north onto Bridge Street.
This 2,000-acre ranch is home to Covell's California Clydesdales, the
largest private breeder of Clydesdale horses in the Western United States.
The large, peaceful horses made famous by a certain American beer
company roam in 100-acre meadows overlooking the Pacific Ocean.

Jim Covell has been raising Clydesdales since 1978. He moved his
operation to Cambria from Southern California in 1998. Today the working
ranch with a history of turning out award-winning teams offers tours to
groups of four or more by appointment only.

Nitwit Ridge (aka Nitt Witt Ridge)
881 Hillcrest Drive
(805) 927-2690
$$$
*From Highway 1, turn east onto Main Street, then left onto Sheffield, left
onto Cornwall and then right onto Hillcrest Drive.*
For many, this structure behind chain-link fencing will seem like nothing
but a pile of garbage loosely connected by smears and plops of cement. For
others, Arthur Harold Beal's lifelong construction project and home may
seem resourceful, even innovative.

Once the city's junk man, Beal, aka Tinkerpaw, called this block home from 1928 to 1989. He used toilet seats as picture frames, perhaps as much for political commentary as utility. Magazine wallpaper, plentiful outhouses and a cascading fountain made of sinks and bathtubs offer glimpses of his artsy side.

Locals differ over what the future should hold for this home made of pipe, beer cans, abalone shells, bottlecaps and other castoffs. For now, it's a registered California State Historical Landmark (No. 939) as a notable 20th Century folk art environment. Public tours are available regularly, but call for current schedule, and keep a close eye on children.

LEFFINGWELL LANDING offers views, beach access, shade, grass and picnic benches.

Chapter 13

San Simeon & Coastal Points North

This world-famous stretch of scenic Highway 1 is home to one of the country's most-visited tourist attractions: Hearst Castle. It also includes countless coves, sandy beaches, and historic points of interest. Bring binoculars for viewing plentiful wildlife, a picnic and jackets; brisk ocean breezes often blow along this stretch.

Written directions for each entry are unnecessary since all publicly accessible properties are directly off Highway 1.

ARTS

National Geographic IMAX Theatre
Hearst Castle Visitors Center
Highway 1 about 7 miles north of Cambria
(805) 927-6811
www.ngtheater.com
$

The gigantic screen of IMAX fame offers regular showings of the Hearst Castle history and construction. Movies start hourly at 8:15 a.m. off season, more regularly during high season. The theater has also been used for special showings of other IMAX presentations.

The lobby features exhibits highlighting county history and art. Access to the lobby exhibits is free.

HISTORY

Hearst Castle
Highway 1 about 7 miles north of Cambria
(800) 444-4445 (tour reservation)
www.hearstcastle.com
$$-$$$

Make reservations at least 10 days in advance if you're planning to tour this 90,000-square-foot home atop rolling coastal mountain foothills overlooking the San Simeon coastline.

It doesn't take a love of architecture, theater, sculpture, tapestry or wine to enjoy William Randolph Hearst's dream home. In fact, Hearst Castle, with its 56 bedrooms, 61 bathrooms, 41 fireplaces, 19 sitting rooms, three pools, tennis courts and zoo, seems a bit much, to say the least.

If the sight of all this development sickens the heart of some visitors, a stop in the sitting room of Casa del Mar holds the cure: a view that lifts the soul. Golden waves of grassland flow down the rolling foothills to sweeping views of the San Simeon coastline and Pacific Ocean. It's a view that has gone largely unchanged since George Hearst, William Randolph Hearst's father, began acquiring the land in 1865.

These days thousands of visitors each year pull off scenic Highway 1 into the ample parking lot at the castle's visitors' center. They meander through the gift shops, past the snack bar and National Geographic IMAX Theater to take bus rides up the hill. Once atop "La Cuesta Encantada" – the enchanted hill, as William Randolph Hearst called it – well-schooled castle docents provide a walking history of the property and its key players. They all have the details of their walking lectures down pat, but they are also open to questions, and seem to know all of the answers.

No single tour covers the entire 127-acre residential property. Instead, the hilltop estate is divided into four daily tours. Some cover portions of the large house, Casa Grande, while others focus on the wine cellar and gardens or the smaller Casa del Mar where younger Hearst spent his final days. All tours include stops at the absolutely magnificent 104-foot-long Neptune Pool.

The Hearst family enjoyed the property for more than half a century as a relatively rugged campsite where canvas tents atop platforms provided the peak of luxury. It wasn't until after 1919 when William Randolph inherited the 250,000-acre estate from his mother, Phoebe Apperson Hearst, that big changes began on the hill. It was then that the younger Hearst contracted with Julia Morgan for the construction of something a bit more comfortable.

George Hearst built his fortune in mining and ranching. Docents report that Hearst hoped his only child would take over those lucrative businesses, but William Randolph was only interested in taking over the family's newspaper – The San Francisco Examiner.

Young Hearst built that single holding into a media empire that helped fund his 28-year love affair with the mountaintop project. Throughout construction, Hearst lived on the hill and served as editor-in-chief of his growing newspaper and magazine empire. Docents point out the desks at which Hearst read each publication when the ink was hardly dry – one at

PIEDRAS BLANCAS, the white rocks, have served as nautical landmarks for centuries.

the foot of his enormous bed; another in the 4,000-plus-book library; others offering scenic views with a simple lift of his chin.

It is little wonder the property was so loved not only by Hearst, but also by visitors. Consideration was given not only to creating a picturesque, inviting atmosphere in the development of well-tended gardens, but Hearst and Morgan aspired to appeal to the artist, athlete and entertainer in each of his guests. He commissioned replicas of great sculptures and the construction of elaborately decorated swimming pools, complete with semi-private dressing rooms.

It is also little wonder that by the late 1930s Hearst's bankroll began to diminish and work on the castle project came to a standstill. In 1957, the Hearst Corporation deeded the castle and adjacent property to the State of California, and today is one of the largest of 5,000 historic "house museums" in the country.

The Hearst Corporation presented the property to the state in 1958 as a memorial. It has since been designated California State Historic Monument No. 6405.

Hearst Castle Visitors Center
Highway 1 about 7 miles north of Cambria
FREE!

Located on the marine terrace well below William Randolph Hearst's castle is a large visitors center. Docent-led tours leave from this center, but it also serves as a free informational center with views of the castle, picnic areas and hugely overpriced, mediocre food. This is also the staging area for docent-led tours of Piedras Blancas Light Station.

Sebastian Store
San Simeon Road
(805) 927-4217
www.ohp.parks.ca.gov
FREE!
From Highway 1 turn west toward Wm. Randolph Hearst Memorial Beach.
The oldest store building along the county's north coast still stands, though half a mile from its original location which was at Whaling Point. The store was built in the 1860s, and moved to its present location in 1878. The Sebastian family continues to offer just what travelers might need.

NATURE
California Coastal National Monument Discovery Center
William Randolph Hearst Memorial State Beach
5 miles south of Hearst Castle on Highway 1
(831) 372-6105
www.blm.gov/ca/pa/coastal_monument/
FREE!

In January 2000, the entire length of California's coastline was designated the California Coastal National Monument in an effort to preserve islands, rocks, exposed reefs and pinnacles. The Discovery Center, scheduled to open in July 2006, is designed to provide public education about the shore and waters extending 12 nautical miles into the Pacific Ocean.

Piedras Blancas elephant seals

Point Piedras Blancas, 11.7 miles north of Cambria on Hwy 1

www.elephant seal.org

(805) 924-1628

☛ FREE!

A pair of two-ton elephant seal bulls lunge toward each other. Their bodies slam together, emitting a dull thud. Before backing away, they bite savagely at each other's neck as they battle for the harem resting a dozen feet away on shore. Wind-whipped waves crash on sand and rock, threatening the infant seals that are born unable to swim. Some mother seals encourage their babies to move further inland while others struggle to push their sinking babies back to shore. A few others continue in a fruitless search for those seal pups already washed too far out to sea.

January marks birthing season at Piedras Blancas elephant seal rookery. Visitors to this stretch of sand just north of San Simeon can witness first hand the circle of life, for better or worse.

An ELEPHANT SEAL ROOKERY near Piedras Blancas offers a real wildlife experience.

That elephant seals continue to exist is a miracle in itself, docents gleefully explain to visitors. The animals, sought for their blubber, were hunted nearly to extinction as the 19th century drew to its close. Docents say that in 1908, Smithsonian scientists found eight elephant seals on an island of the coast of Mexico. Thinking these were the last of the species, they slaughtered the animals and shipped the remains to the museum for research and display.

Jump ahead to a morning in 1990. A marine biologist researching otters along Central Coast stepped out for his morning walk along the bluffs only to discover more than a dozen elephant seals on shore, Mason said. Those allegedly extinct giants of the sea had survived; even made a comeback.

Today, an estimated 7,000 elephant seals stop at Piedras Blancas each year on their trek between San Nicholas Island off Los Angeles and the Farallon Islands north of San Francisco. They mate here, bear their pups here, molt and learn life lessons here.

Onshore, elephant seals look like large, inanimate blobs of blubber. They spend most of their onshore time resting or nursing their young. Spend a bit more time and you'll see they flip sand onto themselves and each other to keep cool or express nervousness; hear their strange calls to each other; and see them head out to sea to fish, fight or play.

While they appear unable to move quickly on shore, elephant seals can in fact charge quite quickly and forcefully with little or no notice. In years past, uneducated visitors have attempted to place their children on and next to the hulking beasts for photos – a dangerous proposition for man and beast. Fences have been erected to help human visitors keep their distance.

From the inland side of the fence, the docents drop tidbits of information as they walk from visitor to visitor. The female elephant seals are generally only about one-third the weight of their 3,000 to 5,000 pound male counterparts. Babies are 60 pounds at birth and unable to fish or swim. They nurse onshore for three weeks, by which time they have grown to some 200 pounds. The mothers then simply swim away, leaving the babies to learn to swim and fish on their own.

There are no facilities at the viewpoint. Pups remain at the beach through March nursing, weaning, learning to swim and feed before beginning their own migration.

Piedras Blancas Light Station

15950 Cabrillo Highway (Highway 1)

www.ca.blm.gov/bakersfield/pbls/index.html

(805) 927-6811

☞ FREE!/$$

The lighthouse, now under the jurisdiction of the U.S. Bureau of Land Management, served as a beacon to ships passing this rocky coastline from 1875 until 1949 when a storm damaged the lantern room and its original Fresnel lens. The lens was removed, the tower capped and a rotating beacon placed on its top. The station was completely automated in 1975. A two-story

PIEDRAS BLANCAS LIGHT STATION tours offer living history, life science and fun.

Victorian-style home that served as the first keepers' residence was later moved to Cambria to serve as a private home.

The only way to access the lighthouse and the point now is via docent-led tours which depart from Hearst Castle Visitors Center down Highway 1. The 90-minute tours are given on the third Saturday of each month. Docents dress in period clothing and act the part of the lighthouse caretaker, lighthouse mistress and related people of the day. There are also frequent discussions about native flora and fauna, not the least of which is migrating whales that can be seen from this point that juts out into the Pacific Ocean.

Free to children under the age of 16.

W.R. Hearst Memorial State Beach
5 miles south of Hearst Castle on Highway 1
www.slostateparks.com/hearst_memorial
(805) 927-2020
☛ FREE!

Hearst Memorial State Beach was home to William Randolph Hearst's own private pier from whence he stocked his famous hilltop estate. The beach and bay are well protected by San Simeon Point, which makes the area ideal for kayakers.

Hearst's previously private south-facing hideaway protected in its little cove is superb for families. Stretch out on the sand, have a picnic in the grassy park, or grab a rod and take a walk on this 795-foot public pier for a bit of fishing. No license is required, though all fishing regulations are in effect. The area is nice for long walks on the beach, tide pooling, kayaking in the bay and body boarding. This park is open daily until sunset.

San Simeon State Park
5 miles south of Hearst Castle on Highway 1
FREE!

A conservation deal with Hearst Ranch at the turn of the 21st Century added 949 acres to this, one of the oldest state parks in the system. The new portion includes 13 miles of coastline stretching from San Simeon to San Carpoforo Creek just south of the county line. Nearly half a dozen entry points are planned for development in coming years including a turnstile at Arroyo Laguna Seca, a popular windsurfing area. Other access points may include Lone Palm Drive, San Simeon Acres, Arroyo de la Cruz and San Carpoforo Creek. There are rumors that a coastal trail will stretch the entire distance.

Until then, take advantage of the trails, campgrounds and breathtaking scenery throughout the established park areas including: Santa Rosa Creek Natural Preserve, 40 acres of forests and wetlands; San Simeon Natural Preserve, 365 acres of wetlands; and Pa-nu Cultural Preserve, a 13.7-acre archeological site dated to 5,580 years ago.

There are several trails in the park, the most accessible of which is the 3.3-mile trail through San Simeon Natural Preserve and Washburn Campground. It includes views, benches and interpretive signs.

The park also includes San Simeon Creek Campgrounds (115 sites for tents or RVs up to 35 feet, flush toilets, coin-op showers, dump station, pay phones); Washburn Campground (primitive campground 1 mile east of Highway 1, chemical toilets, water spigots, dump station). Check with park staff for junior ranger programs, docent-led hikes and regularly scheduled campfire programs.

Leffingwell Landing Day-use Area
Moonstone Beach Drive
(805) 927-0235
www.parks.ca.gov/?page_id=590
FREE!
From Highway 1 turn west onto Moonstone Beach Drive and proceed north.
Leffingwell Landing in San Simeon State Park north of Moonstone Beach is a grassy bluff top featuring Monterey pines, picnic benches, barbecue grills and restrooms. Families play in the sandy beach below, enjoy picnics in the grass, and watch seals on nearby rocks.

Pico Avenue Coastal Access
Pico Avenue
FREE!
From Highway 1 turn west onto Pico Avenue
This long sandy stretch is also known for its tide pools.

Chapter 14

Santa Margarita

This small town off Highway 101 just north of Cuesta Grade is a stepping off point for backcountry adventures, whether on foot, on horseback, via off-highway vehicle or family van. A handful of locally owned businesses provide gas, food and other basic services. Don't expect any old chain standbys here anytime soon.

LETTERS

Santa Margarita Library
9630 Murphy Ave.
(805) 438-5622
slolibrary.org/branch.htm
FREE!
From Highway 101 turn east onto Highway 58 toward Santa Margarita, turn right onto Yerba Buena Avenue, left onto I Street, then left onto Murphy Avenue.

This branch of the San Luis Obispo County Library system is open from noon to 6 p.m. Mondays through Wednesdays.

NATURE

Blue Sky Gardens
19505 Walnut Ave. (Garden Farms)
(805) 438-5801

Downtown SANTA MARGARITA offers last-chance groceries and a handful of restaurants.

www.blueskygardens.sanityonline.com

FREE!

Hwy 101 to Santa Margarita exit. After passing through Santa Margarita continue 1 mile to Linden. Turn left onto Linden, then follow the posted signs.

This family-owned farm welcomes picnickers to enjoy its lawn or stop by to visit the animals. It also offers special events and pick-your-own fruits and vegetables in season including: blackberries, apples, tomatoes, pears and cherries in June and July; pumpkin patch and haunted house in October. Fresh eggs are also on sale and farm animals are available for viewing.

The owner said she does her best to keep the place organic. No sprays are used on berries, and all weeding is done by hand or by rototilling.

Lazy Arrow Outdoor Adventures

9330 Camatta Creek Road

Between Santa Margarita and California Valley/Carizzo Plain

(805) 238-7324

www.lazyarrow.com

$$$

From Highway 101 take the Highway 58/Santa Margarita exit. Continue on Highway 58 east out of town, through Calf Canyon and past La Panza Road. Turn left onto Shell Creek Road, then right onto Camatta Creek Road.

The 32,000-acre Camatta Ranch offers cattle drives semi-annually, fishing, tours, camping, guesthouse accommodations, barbecues, horseshoes, all by reservation.

Railhead Arena

2750 I Street

(805) 467-3535

$$$

From Highway 101 take the Santa Margarita exit and proceed east toward town. Turn right onto Wilhelmina and follow the road as it curves left and becomes I Street.

The Railhead Riders maintain this arena on leased property. The arena is open for use by members (membership is $100 per year/family; $75 for individuals) on weekdays and odd weekends, and gymkhanas are held here on the second and fourth Saturday of every month. There is no fee to watch.

Rinconada Mine Trail

Connecting Highway 58 to Hi Mountain Ridge

www.slopost.org/rinconada.htm

FREE!

From Highway 101 take the Highway 58/Santa Margarita exit. Continue on Highway 58 east out of town. Continue straight onto West Pozo Road. The trailhead is on the right past Las Pilitas Road.

Hikes into LOS PADRES NATIONAL FOREST
turn up all sorts of surprises.

A strenuous trail to the old Rinconada Mine site offers a good starting or ending point for a full day's adventure for big kids and their adult chaperones. Hike, bike or ride horseback 2 miles up the well-maintained, steep, rugged trail to the ridge. Return via the same trail to the car or turn left on the ridge road and travel 7 miles to Hi Mountain Condor Lookout. Or drop down the other side into picturesque Upper Lopez Canyon via Big Falls or Little Falls trails (no bicycles allowed on these trails). Another option is to make a loop ride of it by traveling up the Rinconada Trail, east along the Hi Mountain Lookout fire road, then north along Hi Mountain Road to Pozo with a paved return to the trailhead.

Santa Margarita Community Forest

2000 block of H St.

(805) 549-9319

www.wmcf.org

FREE!

From Highway 101 take the Highway 58/Santa Margarita exit.

Local residents have worked since 1996 to preserve and augment the trees and native plants throughout Santa Margarita. An easy trail through a small park adjacent to the school offers a brief education about common native plants complete with signage.

Go online for a copy of the group's tree walk map (www.smcf.org/tree_walk). Plans are also in the works for an educational trail on about 15 acres of nearby Santa Margarita Ranch.

Santa Margarita Community Park

Corner of H Street and Estrada Avenue/Highway 58

(805) 781-5930

www.slocountyparks.com/facilities/communityparks.htm

☛ FREE!

From Highway 101 take the Highway 58/Santa Margarita exit.

Don't be fooled by the view from Highway 58. What appears to be a tiny roadside park is actually a surprisingly large park for such a small town.

Amenities include new play structures, a restroom, sandbox, swings, gazebo, a bridge over a seasonal creek, a large turf area, picnic area and large barbecue pit

Santa Margarita Lake Regional Park

4695 Santa Margarita Lake Road

(805) 788-2397; Marina Store (805) 438-1522

www.slocountyparks.org

www.slocountyparks.com/facilities/pools.htm (pool info)

☞ $

From Highway 101 take the Highway 58/Santa Margarita exit. Continue on Highway 58 east out of town. Continue straight onto West Pozo Road, then left onto Santa Margarita Lake Road.

Though most notable for its lake, a key source of water for San Luis Obispo, the 7,100-acre park includes campgrounds, a pool and trails available for hikers, mountain bikers and equestrians. Though no body contact with the water is allowed, the lake is available for boating and fishing. A pool provides summer refreshment from Memorial Day to Labor Day.

The lake was created in 1941 by the construction of Salinas Dam. It originally served as a water source for Camp San Luis Obispo. In 1957 the park opened for boating and fishing. Camping is now available, too, including four campgrounds (Coyote, Roadrunner, Grey Pine and Osprey) as well as two primitive boat-in sites (Sapwi and Khus).

SANTA MARGARITA LAKE offers miles of trails and acres of water for fishing or paddling.

Santa Margarita Natural Area, the primary hiking, biking and horseback riding area, is at the east end of the lake. Take West Pozo Road 8 miles east. Turn left on River Road. The entrance is on the left 2 miles down.

Trails in the area include: Grey Pine Trail, 3.7 miles, moderate, hiking/equestrian; Lone Pine Trail, 2.1 miles, strenuous, hiking/equestrian; Rocky Trail, 2 miles moderate to strenuous, multi-use; Vaca Flat 2.6 miles, easy, multi-use; Lakeside Trail, 1.5 miles, easy, hiking/mountain biking; Valley Oak Trail, 2 miles, moderate, multiuse, access to Blinn and Sandstone trailheads; Blinn Road, 9 miles, moderate to strenuous, multi-use (leads to another 1-mile unnamed trail with views to Cuesta Ridge); Sandstone Trail, 6 miles, moderate to strenuous, multi-use.

Wildflower romp on Shell Creek Road
☛ FREE!

From Highway 101 take the Highway 58/Santa Margarita exit. Continue on Highway 58 east out of town, through scenic Calf Canyon and past La Panza Road. Turn left onto Shell Creek Road.

Some of the most spectacular wildflower viewing in San Luis Obispo County can be found up this rural road north of Los Padres National Forest. The meadows and hillsides explode into a natural bouquet of native flowers. Take the drive in late spring for best viewing.

Tidy tips are among the wildflowers that abound east of SANTA MARGARITA.

Pozo is a gateway to the heart of LOS PADRES NATIONAL FOREST.

Chapter 15

Pozo

Downtown Pozo, such that it is, passes in the blink of an eye. The town, if you can call it that, is only a block long and a block and a half deep if you include the California Department of Forestry Fire Department around the corner from the main street.

Pozo offers a wrinkle in the fabric of normalcy: mountain bikers and dirt bikers rub shoulder to shoulder, little old men out for a Sunday drive play horseshoes with long-haired motorcyclists, children run in the sun or stretch out in the shade of very old oak trees. It's little known, but worth a stop.

NATURE

Hi Mountain Road
(805) 925-9538
www.fs.fed.us/r5/lospadres
FREE!/$

From Highway 101 take the Santa Margarita exit and proceed east through town. Turn right onto Highway 58. About 2 miles out of town the road splits. Don't follow Highway 58 left, but continue straight onto Pozo Road.

Across the headwaters of the Salinas River is a well-established dirt road through Los Padres National Forest. The area includes trails, dirt roads, four-wheel-drive trails, motorcycle trails, campgrounds and a California condor lookout. See entry for Los Padres National Forest in the Arroyo Grande chapter for more details.

Pozo/La Panza OHV area
(805) 925-9538
www.fs.fed.us/r5/lospadres/recreation/ohv/slrd/
$

From Highway 101 take Highway 58 east. Continue well out of Santa Margarita. At the Y, continue straight onto Pozo Road, and continue past the Pozo Saloon.

As motorcycle and four-wheel-drive roads and trails become increasingly scarce on the Central Coast, this area becomes more popular. More than 44 miles of trails lead adventurers into the forest, along ridges and to more remote trailheads for backcountry getaways. The Pozo/La Panza area of the Santa Lucia Ranger District includes 18,867 acres of wild space.

Camping is available at Turkey Flat and Navajo Flat, though there are other smaller sites throughout this recreation area. Trails include the relatively flat La Canada Trail along a riverbottom to the experts-only Stair Steps challenge along Pine Mountain Road.

A sturdy fence keeps motorists along Pine Ridge out of Machesna Mountain Wilderness, home of Castle Crags, a nesting site for the endangered California condor. But the abandoned road makes for an exceptionally pleasant and lengthy hike along the ridge and through Coulter pine forest.

An Adventure Pass is required to stop a motorized vehicle in this area. They are available through local sporting goods stores and the U.S. Forest Service.

OTHER ADVENTURES

Pozo Saloon

90 West Pozo Road

(805) 438-4225

www.pozosaloon.com

☛ FREE!

From Highway 101 take Highway 58 east. Continue well out of Santa Margarita. At the Y, continue straight onto Pozo Road.

To feel this rural community's heartbeat, stop by the saloon. Despite its name, the popular establishment is quite family friendly with good barbecue, cold drinks for all ages, indoor seating and outdoor dining under expansive oak trees. Summer weekends bring live music to the back deck and concerts are held with increasing frequency.

The scenic HI MOUNTAIN TRAIL runs from Hi Mountain Road through Hi Valley and ultimately to Hi Mountain Lookout.

Chapter 16

California Valley/Carrizo Plain

The Carrizo Plain is one of San Luis Obispo County's least traveled, most natural remaining places. The 50-mile-long narrow valley is bordered on the east by the Temblor Range and San Andreas Fault and on the west by the Caliente Range. It is home to expansive ranches, secluded homes and Carrizo Plain National Monument.

The peace of the valley is timeless, but some of the best seasons to visit are winter for raptor and sand hill crane viewing and late spring when the valley explodes into a bouquet of wildflowers.

Though the valley is expansive, services here are very limited. There is no gas station and a restaurant near the valley's centrally located fire station sometimes provides food and even local musical entertainment. Call ahead.

LETTERS

Simmler Public Library
13080 Soda Lake Road
(805) 475-2603
slolibrary.org/branch.htm
FREE!
From 101, take the Santa Margarita/Highway 58 exit and head east through town. Just past downtown Santa Margarita, turn right across the railroad tracks and follow Highway 58 about 35 miles to California Valley. Turn south onto Soda Lake Road.
A branch of the San Luis Obispo County library system. Open Wednesdays.

NATURE

Carrizo Plain National Monument
Between Highway 166 and Highway 58 both sides of Soda Lake Road
(805) 475-2131 (seasonal)
www.ca.blm.gov/bakersfield/recopportunitiescpna.html
☛ FREE!
From 101, take the Santa Margarita/Highway 58 exit and head east through town. Just past downtown Santa Margarita, turn right across the railroad tracks and follow Highway 58 about 35 miles to California Valley. Turn south onto Soda Lake Road.

The 250,000-acre monument was set aside in 2001 after generations of families farmed and ranched in this remote valley that separates the coast from the central valley. It is home to more than half a dozen species of unusual, endangered or threatened animals including: San Joaquin kit fox, the California condor, the blunt-nosed leopard lizard, the giant kangaroo rat, the San Joaquin antelope squirrel, the longhorn fairy shrimp and the vernal pool fairy shrimp. The list of plants growing in the valley is huge, but unusual, rare and endangered specimens found here include: astragalus, spiny-sepaled button celery, pale-yellow layia, forked fiddleneck, Jared's peppergrass, Lost Hills crownscale, San Joaquin bluecurls, Hoover's eriastrum, cottony buckwheat, temblor buckwheat, hollisteria, gypsum-loving larkspur, oval-leaved snapdragons, stinkbells, Kern tarplant, California jewelflower, Hoover's wooly-star and San Joaquin woolythreads (source: BLM Bakersfield office).

The valley is rife with evidence that the Chumash, Yokuts and Silanan tribes called this valley home, the most publicly accessible of which is Painted Rock. From Highway 58, travel south on Soda Lake Road 14 miles to the Goodwin Education Center on Painted Rock Road. The center is open winter and spring Thursdays through Sunday from 9 a.m. to 4 p.m., though it has been known to close early if no visitors are on site. Access to the rock is limited March 1 through late May when it is closed until July 15. Climbing on, touching or otherwise defacing the rock and its artwork is prohibited, as are bicycles, dogs or any other pets.

For a long scenic drive in good weather, take the 70-mile Soda Lake, Elkhorn Plain, and Seven Mile roads loop. These roads are unpaved and the

The Caliente Ridge trek involves plenty of steady climbs and decents before reaching CALIENTE PEAK, the highest peak in San Luis Obispo County

clay from which they are carved is dangerously slippery when wet. In good weather, they provide sufficient surface for most street vehicles and provide access to some of the monument's official points of interest. They include the Goodwin Center and Painted Rock as well as:

Soda Lake Boardwalk – *About 9 miles south of Highway 58 on the east side of Soda Lake Road.* A short dirt path leads to a wooden boardwalk that extends along the oft-squishy banks of one of the largest remaining natural alkali wetlands in California.

Soda Lake Viewpoint – *About 9 miles from Highway 58 turn right onto the dirt spur road.* The road circles around the back of a small hill where there is ample parking. A short uphill hike on a dirt path leads to a saddle between two low peaks. The splendid view of the valley includes the Soda Lake Boardwalk almost directly across Soda Lake Road. For more expansive views, continue north or south along the ridge trail to its termini where additional information signs are posted.

Wallace Creek – *From Highway 58, turn right on Seven Mile Road. Continue about ½ mile, then turn left onto Elkhorn Road and continue south about 4 miles to a clearly marked parking area.* Interpretive signs along this out-and-back trail explain how and why Wallace Creek shifted 30 feet in a single day as the San Andreas Fault over which it passes moved in a massive quake. The dirt trail is not stroller friendly but does include a child-friendly mellow climb.

F Caliente Ridge/Caliente Peak
Selby Road & Caliente Ridge Road
(661) 391-6000
www.blm.gov/ca//bakersfield/calientemtn.html
FREE!

From Highway 58 turn south onto Soda Lake Road and continue about 15 miles. Turn west onto Selby Road and follow the dirt road about 5 miles to the locked gate at the ridge.

This rural ridge offers plentiful quiet saddles and peaks with views spanning as far east as the Sierra Nevada and west to the Sierra Madre. Traffic is minimal here due to extreme off-the-beaten-path location, but the ridge is readily accessible via a well-maintained dirt road.

Once parked along the ridge, take a rugged stroller, mountain bike or hike along the ridge as it dips and rises 8 miles east to Caliente Peak, the highest peak in San Luis Obispo County. Reaching the peak is not for the average youngster, but keen teens may be able to tackle it. The ridge offers plenty of beautiful picnic spots, birding opportunities and family photo ops along the way.

CHARLES PADDOCK ZOO is a highlight for young children visiting Atascadero.

Chapter 17

Atascadero

Once a small town serving cowboys in northern San Luis Obispo County, Atascadero is a growing family-friendly community. Coastal mountain ranges protect this and other North County communities from the Pacific's marine layer, bringing much warmer summer weather than in communities in the south county or along the coast.

ARTS

Century Cinemas
6905 El Camino Real
(805) 227-2172
$$

From northbound Highway 101 take the Highway 41/Morro Road exit, turn right at the end of the ramp onto Highway 41, then left onto El Camino Real. From southbound Highway 101 take the Traffic Way exit, turn left onto Traffic Way, then right onto El Camino Real.

This six-screen theater has all the latest Hollywood blockbusters.

LETTERS

Atascadero – Martin Polin Regional Library
6850 Morro Road
(805) 461-6161
slolibrary.org/branch.htm
FREE!

From Highway 101 take the Highway 41/Morro Road exit. Turn west onto Morro Road.

A branch of the San Luis Obispo City-County Library system. Active supporters have been raising funds and pushing for a move to a larger facility, but there is no date certain for the move.

HISTORY

Atascadero Administration Rotunda
6500 Palma Ave
(805) 461-5000
www.atascadero.org/?page_id=2786
FREE!

From northbound Highway 101 take the Highway 41/Morro Road exit, turn right at the end of the ramp onto Highway 41, then left onto El Camino Real, then right onto East Mall Road and then left onto Palma Ave.. From southbound Highway 101 take the Traffic Way exit, turn left onto Traffic Way, then right onto Palma Avenue.

Northeast of the city's sunken garden, just off El Camino Real is one of Atascadero's most historical structures. The rotunda, built from 1914 to 1918 of reinforced concrete and locally produced brick, has served as the headquarters for Edward G. Lewis's model community, Atascadero Colony as the town was originally known. The building has also served as a private school for boys, a veterans' memorial building, county offices and city offices. The site was named California Historic Landmark No. 958 before it was heavily damaged in the 2003 Paso Robles earthquake, leaving the Atascadero Historical Museum which it houses closed indefinitely.

Amigos de Anza and Paso Robles Trails Association
Multiple accesses
(805) 461-5000
www.nps.gov/juba
FREE!

Pick up a trail guide from Atascadero, Paso Robles and San Luis Obispo chambers of commerce or Atascadero Recreation Department to begin exploring the route traveled by Juan Bautista de Anza in 1775-76. He led 30 soldiers and their families along this trail in search of a route to the San Francisco Bay. Today, the city welcomes visitors to travel more than 5 miles of trail along the Salinas River by foot, bicycle or horseback. No motorized vehicles are allowed.

Since the total length of the trail is more than 1,000 miles, the parks service offers an online junior ranger program. For more information go to www.anzajuniorranger.org.

NATURE

Anza Arena
East of 905 El Camino Real
www.atascadero.org/cs
FREE!

From Highway 101 take Santa Cruz Road east, turn left onto El Camino Real.

This public equestrian arena includes ample parking for trucks and trailers and provides access to the Juan Bautista de Anza Trail. The arena is regularly used for practice and gymkhanas.

Atascadero High School Swimming Pool
1 High School Hill
(805) 470-3472

$

*From Highway 101 take Traffic Way exit, turn west onto Traffic Way/
Santa Lucia Road, immediately left onto Ardilla Road, then right onto
Atascadero Mall which becomes High School Hill Road.*

The high school's pool is sometimes used for summer lessons and
recreational swimming through the city recreation department.

Atascadero Lake Park

9305 Pismo Avenue

(805) 461-5000

www.atascadero.org/cs

☞ FREE!

From Highway 101 head west on Highway 41/Morro Road.

The namesake of this 25-acre park is open year round for rowing, paddling
and fishing, but no swimming. Large play structures, swings, sand pits and
wooded lawns provide active entertainment. The park also boasts multiple
picnic areas, large barbecue pits, restrooms, a gazebo, and a public wading
pool that is open summers only.

The park is a popular place for parties, but reservations are required to
ensure access to a group area. The city also hosts free public concerts in the
park every Tuesday evening during summer months. The neighboring
Charles Paddock Zoo is an added attraction.

ATASCADERO LAKE PARK offers paddling, swinging, walking and plenty of waterfowl.

Kayaks are available for rent during spring weekends and all summer. Call (805) 441-7463 for current hours and rates.

Atascadero Youth Recreation Center
Traffic Way at Bajada Avenue
(805) 470-3472
www.atascadero.org/cs
FREE!

From Highway 101 take the Traffic Way exit and proceed east on Traffic Way.

This 19,000-square-foot facility set to open in 2007 will include a gymnasium, arts and crafts room, dance and exercise rooms, teen center and café. The center will be adjacent to Traffic Way Park and a planned swimming complex on two additional acres.

Chalk Mountain Golf Course
10000 El Bordo Rd.
(805) 466-8848
www.chalkmountaingolf.com
$$-$$$

From Highway 101 take the Santa Rosa Road exit and turn east. Turn right onto El Camino Real, then left onto El Bordo Avenue.

This 18-hole public golf course offers year-round play, a driving range, club rental and an onsite golf pro. Oak trees line the narrow fairways of this hilly course bordering Heilmann Regional Park.

Green Acres Lavender Farm
8865 San Gabriel Road
(805) 466-0837
www.greenacreslavenderfarm.com
FREE!

From Highway 101 take the Santa Rosa Road exit and proceed west on Santa Rosa Road. Turn left onto Atascadero Avenue, and then right onto San Gabriel Road.

This family-run lavender farm near Charles Paddock Zoo offers public tours, workshops and other events among more than 12,000 lavender plants. Call for appointment.

Happy Grapes
13005 Salinas Road
(805) 462-0347
FREE!

From Highway 101 take the Santa Barbara Road exit and head west. Turn right onto El Camino Real, left onto Santa Clara Road, then left onto Salinas Road.

Pick your own Thompson grapes at this farm that opens to the public September and October weekends.

Heilmann Regional Park

9400 El Bordo Avenue

(805) 781-5930

www.slocountyparks.com

☞ FREE!

From Highway 101 take the Santa Rosa Road exit and turn east. Turn right onto El Camino Real, then left onto El Bordo Avenue.

Although the park is well signed, visitors are unlikely to happen upon this expansive stretch of green hidden from the main drag by a neighborhood, hill and dale.

The oak-studded rolling hills of this 37-acre park adjacent to Chalk Mountain Golf Course feature a flying disc golf course, lighted tennis courts, off-leash dog park, play structures, swings, restrooms and spraying jets of cool water that invite visitors to splash throughout the hot summer months. The park also includes three main trails including: Blue Oak Trail, an easy, 1.3-mile multiuse trail; Jim Green Trail, a 1.7-mile, moderately strenuous trail that connects hikers and equestrian users to the park from neighborhoods to the north; and a stretch of the 5.8-mile-long Juan Bautista de Anza Trail, an easy multi-use trail.

Kennedy Club Fitness Center Pool

3534 El Camino Real

(805) 466-6775

www.kennedyclubs.com/Atascadero/aquatics.htm

$$$

From Highway 101 take the Del Rio Road exit east, then turn right onto El Camino Real.

This pool offers a youth swim team, water polo team, springboard diving lessons and water safety courses including lifeguard training. It is also available for lap swim with reduced prices for members.

Paloma Creek Park

11665 Viejo Camino

(805) 461-5000

www.atascadero.org/cs

FREE!

From Highway 101 take the Atascadero Road / Santa Barbara Road exit. Turn east onto Santa Barbara Road. Jog slightly left across El Camino Real and continue east on Santa Barbara Road, then turn left onto Viejo Camino.

This 23-acre neighborhood park offers a picnic area, play structures, soccer fields, two softball fields, little league fields, horsehoe pits, a large barbecue pit, and restrooms. It also includes Miles Wemp Arena, a public equestrian arena.

Scott's Iris Gardens
14605 Chispa Road
(805) 461-3270
www.GardenEureka.com/scott
FREE!

South Atascadero off El Camino Real. 2 miles north of Santa Margarita turn east on Asuncian Rd and north on Chispa Rd, 1/4 mile on right.

This commercial nursery welcomes the public in its demonstration and educational gardens April through June. Visitors are also invited to commune with farm animals living on site.

Stadium Park
Off Capistrano Avenue near Highway 41
(805) 461-5000
www.atascadero.org/cs
FREE!

From Highway 101 take the Highway 41/Morro Road exit. Turn east onto Highway 41, then left onto Capistrano Avenue.

A natural amphitheatre in the middle of town.

Sunken Gardens Park
6500 block El Camino Real
(805) 461-5000
www.atascadero.org/cs
FREE!

From Highway 101 take the Traffic Way exit, turn east onto Traffic Way, then right onto El Camino Real.

The two-acre park in front of the city's rotunda building offers plenty of room to play tag, enjoy a fountain and view public art, but its proximity to a major thoroughfare may deter families with small children.

Traffic Way Park
5599 Traffic Way
(805) 461-5000
www.atascadero.org/cs
FREE!

From Highway 101 take the Traffic Way exit, and turn east onto Traffic Way.

This is a three-acre park that offers two softball fields, a children's play area with structures, and restrooms.

OTHER ADVENTURES

Beatie Skate Park

5493 Traffic Way

(805) 470-3472

www.atascadero.org/cs

FREE!

From Highway 101 take Traffic Way east four blocks.

The only indoor skate park in San Luis Obispo County features modular ramps, a lounge area, a small concession stand, and restrooms. Pads, signed waiver forms, and helmets with straps are required for skaters of all ages. The park is generally open during the school year from 3 p.m. to 6 p.m. Monday through Friday, 10 a.m. to 3 p.m. Saturday and 1 p.m. to 4 p.m. Sunday. Call for extended summer hours and skate camp offerings.

Charles Paddock Zoo

9305 Pismo Avenue

(805) 461-5080

www.atascadero.org/cs/zoo

$

From Highway 101 head west on Highway 41/Morro Road.

For decades this five-acre zoo adjacent to Atascadero Lake Park has given children an up close and personal view of animals from forests, deserts, mountains and farms. With about 100 animals, relatively small enclosures and a bit of running room, the zoo is fine for small children, but is less exciting for bigger kids.

The zoo hosts special events throughout the year including zoo camps and holiday events. Call for current offerings.

There are loads of agricultural education opportunities in Templeton.
JACK CREEK FARM offers hands-on activities for children.

Chapter 18

Templeton

Tucked off today's beaten path is an old-town community made up of residents who know how to get things done. Though small in population, the community is home to amenities often not found in cities twice its size.

ARTS

Templeton Performing Arts Center
1200 South Main Street
(805) 423-2471
www.tusdnet.k12.ca.us/pac
FREE!-$$$
From Highway 101 take Vineyard Road east, then turn right onto South Main Street.
This 340-seat theater offers public performances by theater arts students at Templeton High School and arts organizations throughout the area. Call for current program, prices and rules regarding young children.

LETTERS

Templeton Library
Near the intersection of Vineyard and Main streets
(805) 434-1119
FREE!
Templeton has been without a library since 1977, but an active support group has raised significant funds and interest in building a new library. No construction date had been set as of this first edition printing.

HISTORY

Templeton Historical Museum
309 Main St.
(805) 434-0807
www.templetonmuseum.org
FREE!
From Highway 101 take the Vineyard Road exit. Proceed east on Vineyard Road, and then turn left onto Main Street.
The Templeton Historical Museum Society operates this non-profit museum that focuses on the lives and times of Templeton area residents. The

original museum is operated in a historic home built at the turn of the 19th Century. An 1886 Southern Pacific Railroad warehouse building houses large equipment including antique cars, trucks and buggies. Docents open the library Fridays through Sundays from 1 p.m. to 4 p.m.

NATURE

Bethel Road Park

300 block of South Bethel Road

www.templetoncsd.org

(805) 434-4900

FREE!

From Highway 101 take the Las Tablas Road exit and turn west onto Las Tablas Road, then left onto South Bethel Road.

This 5-acre community park offers running space including a soccer field, restrooms, playground with structures, open turf and basketball hoops.

Chesebrough Farm

790 Moss Lane

(805) 434-0843

FREE!

Exit Highway 101 at Vineyard and head east. When Vineyard curves sharply left and becomes El Pomar, continue straight onto graded-dirt Moss Lane and continue a mile and a bit to the farm.

This working cow-calf operation on a century-old farm is open to the public daily in October from 9 a.m. to 5 p.m. The Chesebroughs welcome visitors to

CHESEBROUGH FARM opens its doors in October for pumpkin season and farm tours.

look at fields in different stages of cultivation, growth and harvest, the refurbished barn (including original milking stanchions), vintage machines, big tractors, farm stand and pumpkin patch. Call ahead to arrange guided tour.

Duveneck Natural Area

490 Vaquero Drive
(805) 781-5200
www.slocountyparks.com
FREE!

Take Highway 101 to El Pomar. Turn east and continue on El Pomar, then turn left onto Vaquero Drive.

This 90-acre property, donated by the family of Bernard H. (Barney) Duvenek, is slated to become a park, most likely with an emphasis on agricultural education. No opening date has been scheduled. Call for current developments.

Ever's Sports Park

East end of Gibson Road
(805) 434-4900
www.templetoncsd.org
FREE!

From Highway 101 take the Las Tablas Road exit and turn east onto Las Tablas Road. Turn left onto Old Country Road, then right onto Gibson Road.

This 8-acre park includes baseball, softball and T-ball fields, soccer fields, concession stand, and restrooms, all under lights.

Hollyhock Farms

200 Hollyhock Lane
(805) 239-4713
www.hollyhock-farm.com
FREE!

From Highway 101 take the Vineyard exit and turn east onto Vineyard. Veer left onto El Pomar Road and continue about 4 miles to Hollyhock Lane. Turn left onto the lane and continue another mile to the farm.

Visitors are invited to watch organic farming in action, pick floral bouquets June through December or enjoy an overnight farm stay by reservation any time. The farm includes 80 chickens, Jacob sheep and organic-farming education.

Jack Creek Farms

4665 Jack Creek Road
(805) 238-3799
www.jackcreekfarms.com

FREE!

From Highway 101 turn west onto Highway 46 and continue 6 miles to the farm.

This working family farm grows pumpkins, heirloom tomatoes, antique apples and other produce and offers pick-your-own flowers and berries from late June through mid-November. Families are welcome to use the picnic tables and children's play area, visit farm animals or view antique farm machinery. The farm is also home to the annual Harvest Festival complete with its Old-Fashioned Threshing Bee in early October.

Templeton Community Center

601 S. Main Street

(805) 434-4900

www.templetoncsd.org

FREE!

From Highway 101 take the Vineyard Road exit. Proceed east on Vineyard Road, and then turn left onto Main Street.

This 2,525-square-foot building is a hub of activity. The property includes the town's skate park and a community garden. The facility's meeting rooms are available for public use by reservation.

Templeton Community Garden Project

601 S. Main Street

(805) 434-4900

www.templetoncsd.org

FREE!

From Highway 101 take the Vineyard Road exit. Proceed east on Vineyard Road, and then turn left onto Main Street.

Residents of Templeton are invited to adopt any of 30 garden plots behind the Community Center.

Templeton Community Park

Fifth and Main streets

(805) 781-5930

www.templetoncsd.org

☛ FREE!

From Highway 101 take the Vineyard Road exit. Proceed east on Vineyard Road, and then turn left onto Main Street.

This good old-fashioned city center park features an entire city block of fun for the family: plenty of grassy space for throwing a ball or playing tag, play structures, swings, a gazebo, picnic tables, large barbecue pit and restrooms. A public pool in the park offers free swimming during the hot summer months, thanks to local Lions Clubs that help fund pool operation. A fire department located directly across the street from the park will serve as an added bonus for families whose kids just can't get enough of those big ol' trucks.

Templeton Park Pool

6th and Old Country Road in Templeton Community Park

(805) 781-5930

www.slocountyparks.com/facilities/pools.htm

FREE!

From Highway 101 take the Vineyard Road exit. Proceed east on Vineyard Road, turn left onto Old Country Road.

The Lions Club adopted the pool in recent years, ensuring the plunge's future and providing free swimming for all. Open Memorial Day to Labor Day.

Templeton Skate Park

599 Main Street

(805) 434-4900

www.templetoncsd.org

☞ FREE!

From Highway 101 take the Vineyard Road exit. Proceed east on Vineyard Road, and then turn left onto Main Street.

Helmets and pads are required at this free, 10,000-square-foot concrete park featuring rails, half pipes and two bowls. Hours vary with the local school schedule. Basically, if school's in session, the park is closed. During summer hours the park is generally open from sun up to sundown.

Chapter 19

Paso Robles

Many people still think of Paso Robles as a dusty cow town, home to the California Mid-State Fair, kids in cowboy hats and jeans, but little more. In fact, Paso Robles is in the middle of a revival complete with upscale restaurants and shops and the renovation of some of its historic places.

Images of cowboys, cattle and working horses permeate the 200-year-old Central Coast city, from Cowboy Café to Western Art Gallery and on toward the fairgrounds. Look closer and you'll find a wine bar, museums, haute cuisine, a rejuvenated park and revived downtown event calendar.

ARTS

Call-Booth House Gallery
1315 Vine St.
(805) 238-5473
FREE!

Paso Robles City Park is home to the CARNEGIE LIBRARY, play structures and annual

From northbound Highway 101 take the Spring Street exit and proceed north on Spring Street, turn left onto 14th Street, then right onto Vine Street. From southbound Highway 101 take the 24th Street exit and turn west onto 24th Street, then left onto Vine Street.

As if this Queen Anne style house weren't enough reason to visit, the Paso Robles Art Association now uses the home as its premier gallery. The gallery is open from 11 a.m. to 3 p.m. Wednesdays through Sundays.

The house, listed in the National Register of Historic Places, was built in 1893 by John Burkett for Dr. Samuel Johnson Call. Call was a surgeon and famous member of the Revenue Cutter Service. It was with that service that he traveled to the Arctic to help rescue sailors on whaling ships that had been trapped in ice during an exceptionally early winter. His work on the Overland Relief Expedition of 1897-98 earned him a Congressional Medal of Honor.

Park Cinemas

1100 Pine St.

(805) 227-2172

$$

From northbound Highway 101 take the Spring Street exit and proceed north on Spring Street, and then turn right onto Pine Street.. From southbound Highway 101 take the Riverside Ave./Pine Street exit, proceed north onto Pine Street.

A nine-screen movie theater offering all the latest Hollywood has to offer.

Pioneer Players

1339 Riverside Ave.

(805) 239-1638

www.pioneerplayers.org

$$-$$$

From southbound Highway 101 take the 16th Street exit, turn right onto Riverside Road. From northbound Highway 101 turn east onto 24th Street, then turn left onto Riverside Road.

This community theater has offered public performance for varying ages since 1965. Shows are regularly sold out. Watch local calendars for current offerings or call ahead.

LETTERS

Paso Robles City Library

1000 Spring Street

(805) 237-3870

www.prcity.com/government/departments/library/

FREE!

From Highway 101 southbound take the Pine Street exit. Turn left onto 10th Street then right onto Spring Street. From northbound Highway 101 take the Spring Street exit and proceed straight to the library.

The library offers toddler story time, preschool story time, Homework Helpers tutoring program and Grandparents and Books Program. Open

ESTRELLA ADOBE CHURCH offers a bit of local history.

Mondays through Fridays from 10 a.m. to 8 p.m., Saturdays 10 a.m. to 5 p.m. Closed Sundays.

Paso Robles City Library Study Center
3201 Spring Street
(805) 237-4743
www.prcity.com/government/departments/library/
FREE!
From Highway 101 take Exit 232 and proceed south on Spring Street.
This facility includes tables, chairs and a few computers for student use after school. While no tutors are employed here, students are welcome to bring in their own tutors. Open Monday through Thursday from 2:30 p.m. to 5:30 p.m.

HISTORY

Estrella Adobe Church
Airport Road 2.5 miles north of Highway 46
(805) 467-3357
www.rios-caledoniaadobe.org/index_files/Page433.htm
FREE!
From Highway 101 turn east onto Highway 46, then left onto Airport Road.
This adobe, built in 1878, was the first Protestant church in northern San Luis Obispo County. The grounds are open to the public, but there are no public amenities. Although the 75-seat adobe is available for special events by reservation, its doors are not generally open to the public. One exception is the annual memorial service held each May to honor the pioneers.

Estrella Warbirds Museum
4251 Dry Creek Road
(805) 227-0440
www.ewarbirds.org
☛ FREE!
From Highway 101 turn east onto Highway 46, turn left onto Airport Road, then right onto Dry Creek Road.
More than 200 volunteers have developed this private museum of historic aircraft, military machinery and war-era memorabilia ranging from pictures to uniforms. An onsite reference library of some 5,000 books documents American involvement in war around the world.

The museum was named after the World War II U.S. Army Air Corps P-38 training base once situated on the adjacent Paso Robles Municipal Airport. Estrella Warbirds operates on land leased from the city and most of the aircraft on display are on loan from the U.S. Naval Museum in Pensacola, Florida.

The official hours are Saturdays 10 a.m. to 3 p.m. and Sundays noon to 3 p.m., but weekday tours are available by appointment, and special events are also scheduled occasionally throughout the year.

The Estrella Squadron meets the first Wednesday of each month at 7 p.m. in the meeting hall on site. Young people are welcome to take part in most aspects of the organization, including aircraft renovation.

Pioneer Museum
2010 Riverside Ave.
(805) 239-4556
www.prpioneermuseum.org
☛ FREE!

From southbound Highway 101 take the 16th Street exit, turn right onto Riverside Road. From northbound Highway 101 turn east onto 24th Street, then turn left onto Riverside Road.

Spending an entire afternoon in and around the museum adjacent to Pioneer Park should be no problem for most families given this nonprofit's extensive collection of Americana.

The entrance hall features exhibits displaying life as it was: a print shop, bank, sporting goods store, creamery, gun shop, post office, hospital, mercantile and cattle camp. There's plenty of taxidermy, exhibits about area mining efforts and the historic Geneseo Schoolhouse which houses an exhibit of early American public schooling.

The museum claims its barbed wire collection is the largest in the Western U.S. It hangs on a wall in the neighboring building which also houses a fine collection of vintage carriages, buggies, cars and trucks including a 1911 Maxwell.

Open afternoons Thursday through Sunday.

NATURE

Barney Schwartz Park
2970 Union Road
(805) 237-3991
www.prcity.com/government/departments/recreation/facilities
☛ FREE!

From Highway 101 take Highway 46 east. Turn right onto Union Road which splits immediately south of Highway 46. Take Union Road to the left.

This 40-acre modern sports park includes four baseball/softball diamonds, four soccer/football fields, a lake, group picnic areas, two concession stands, three large play structure areas, a small lake and loads of walking paths.

Berry Hill Farm
4855 Linne Road
(805) 238-3612

FREE!

From Highway 101 northbound take Spring Street, turn right onto Niblick Road. From southbound Highway 101 take Paso Robles Street exit and proceed straight, turn right onto Creston Road, then left onto Niblick Road. Continue east on Niblick Road as it jogs and becomes Linne Road.

Let the kids pick their own olallieberries, Fuji apples and Granny Smith apples when the fruit is in season.

Carnegie Library

800 12th Street

(805) 238-4996

FREE!

From Highway 101 turn west onto 13th Street, then left onto Spring Street.

This historic stone structure listed in the National Register of Historic Places was built in 1908 and housed the city's library for 90 years. When the city moved the library to more modern digs, the Paso Robles Historical Society took over the space where it now maintains historical and genealogical records for public reference.

Carnegie Western Art Gallery

800 12th Street

(805) 238-4996

FREE!

From Highway 101 turn west onto 13th Street, then left onto Spring Street.

Down the tiny set of steps to the left of the historic library's main entrance is a small gallery that features original Western art of varying shapes, styles and sizes.

Casa Robles Park

Appaloosa Drive and Palomino Circle

(805) 237-4134

www.prcity.com/government/departments/recreation/facilities

FREE!

From Highway 101 northbound exit onto Spring Street, turn right onto Niblick Road, then left onto Appaloosa Drive. From Southbound Highway 101 exit at Pine Street, turn left onto 4th Street, left onto spring Street, left onto Niblick Road and left onto Appaloosa Drive.

This is a quarter-acre park with a play structure and a bit of grass.

Centennial Park

600 Nickerson Drive

(805) 237-3991

(805) 237-3988 (pool)

www.prcity.com/government/departments/recreation/facilities

FREE!

From Highway 101 turn east onto Highway 46, then right onto River Road, left onto Creston Road and right onto Nickerson Drive.

This 16-acre park includes a gymnasium with basketball court, wading pool, two large group barbeque areas, grassy picnic areas, an amphitheatre, walking paths, two playgrounds, two outdoor half-court basketball courts and four lighted tennis courts. There is also an outdoor pool that operates June through August.

Franklin Hotsprings

3085 Creston Road, Paso Robles

(805) 239-0478

www.franklinhotsprings.com

$-$$

From Highway 101 take the Niblick Road exit in Paso Robles. Turn east onto Niblick Road, and then right onto Creston Road and continue about 2.3 miles to the lakes on the south side of the road.

Franklin Lake Aquaculture Farm is a privately owned hot springs and recreation resort offering opportunities to dip into a pool that is maintained at 98 degrees by nature, fishing in a private lake (no license required), space to run remote control boats and plenty of room for paintball on a designated field of play. The hot springs pool is open daily from 8 a.m. to midnight and occasionally operates on the honor system (just deposit payment on your way to the pool area). The paintball park, open daily 9 a.m. to 4 p.m. in the winter and 9 a.m. until undesignated time in summer, offers paintball equipment rental and sales.

Harris Stage

5995 North River Road

(805) 237-1860

www.harrisstagelines.com

$$$

From Highway 101 turn east onto Highway 46, then left onto North River Road.

This private ranch specializes in the training of horses, but also hosts private events and activities including riding and driving lessons, horse-drawn vehicles for hire (chariots, carriages, hay wagon rides, chuck wagon, stagecoach), parties, school field trips. The ranch also holds cowboy and cowgirl day camps for children ages 7 and up, and overnight camps for children ages 10 to 18. There are also two- and three-day clinics for adults with focuses on horsemanship, driving, and riding.

Hunter Ranch Golf Course

4041 highway 46 East

(805) 237-7444

www.hunterrranchgolf.com

$$$

From Highway 101 take Highway 46 east to the course.

A public/private 18-hole course offers junior lessons, driving range, four putting greens, mini-executive three-hole practice course, golf shop, group barbecue facilities, and Caddie's Grill at the clubhouse. The facility also offers private and group lessons.

The Links Course of Paso Robles

5151 Jardine Road

(805) 227-4567

www.linkscourseatpasorobles.com

$$$

From Highway 101 take Highway 46 east, and then turn left onto Jardine Road.

Play 9 holes or 18 at this par-72 course that features a Scottish-style course and offers junior rates.

Mandella Park

Fairview Lane

(805) 237-4134

www.prcity.com/government/departments/recreation/facilities

FREE!

From Highway 101 take the Highway 46/24th Street exit and head west. Turn right onto Fairview Lane.

A quarter-acre open area is more a green space than a park. There are no amenities here.

Melody Park

North Country Club Drive

(805) 237-4134

www.prcity.com/government/departments/recreation/facilities

FREE!

From northbound Highway 101 take the Spring Street Exit, then turn east onto Niblick Road. From southbound Highway 101 take Pine Street, turn left onto 4th Street, left onto Spring Street, then left onto Niblick Road. From Niblick Road, turn left onto Country Club Drive.

Another quarter-acre park/drainage basin that has included a play structure, but it's on the way out and there are no other amenities here.

Meridian Vineyard

7100 Highway 46 East

(805) 226-7133

www2.ibgcheckout.com/meridian/

☞ **FREE!**

From Highway 101 take Highway 46 east.

While primarily a wine making facility with wine tasting for adults, Meridian Vineyard also features one of the most beautiful public herb gardens in the area. Families are welcome to bring their own picnics and frolic under the oaks, explore the garden or simply enjoy a peaceful day out.

Mount Olive Company

3445 Adelaida Road

(805) 237-0147

www.mtoliveco.com

FREE!

From Highway 101 take the Highway 46/24th Street exit and head west. Veer left onto Adelaida Road.

This certified organic farm turns out seasonal fruits and vegetables including strawberries, olives and more than a dozen types of sprouts from alfalfa to wheatgrass. Free range chickens help keep down pests, and also provide fresh eggs. Fruit orchard and worm farming tours led by super friendly staff are available by appointment 10 a.m. to 7 p.m. Thursdays through Sundays. An organic lunch menu is also featured at the company store where all products grown here are also for sale.

Oak Creek Park

Cedarwood Drive at Creston Road

(805) 237-3991

www.prcity.com/government/departments/recreation/facilities

FREE!

From Highway 101 northbound take Spring Street, turn right onto Niblick Road, then right onto Creston Road. From southbound Highway 101 take Paso Robles Street exit and proceed straight, turn right onto Creston Road.

This 10½-acre park south of Sherwood Park includes a three-quarter-mile lighted walking path, playground, and three small barbecue/picnic areas.

Paso Robles City Park, Carnegie Library and Western Art Museum

Bounded by Spring, 11th, 12th and Pine streets

(805) 238-4103

www.prcity.com/government/departments/recreation/facilities/city-park.asp

☞ **FREE!**

From Highway 101 turn west onto 13th Street, then left onto Spring Street.

While Paso Robles evolves and upgrades, 4.8-acre City Park maintains its hold on our attention with its wooded walks, play structures, historic Carnegie Library and works of art in the Western Art Museum. The park also offers horseshoe pits, picnic tables, a gazebo and restrooms.

Stump art in Paso Robles City Park.

The city sponsors free twilight concerts in the park throughout the summer. Other annual events that call this park home include Pioneer Day, Mid-State Fair Pancake Breakfast, Trading Day, Paso Robles Wine Festival, car shows and 4th of July festivities.

Paso Robles Event Center (aka Mid-State Fairgrounds)
2198 Riverside Ave.
(805) 239-0655
www.midstatefair.com
FREE!-$$$
From Highway 101 turn west onto24th Street, then left onto Riverside Avenue.
This 40-acre facility hosts the California Mid-State Fair each July/August and other special events throughout the year including agricultural exhibitions, equestrian events, concerts and trade shows. Call for current offerings.

Paso Robles Golf Club
1600 Country Club Drive
(805) 238-4722

www.centralcoast.com/pasoroblesgolfclub

$$

From northbound Highway 101 take the Spring Street Exit, then turn east onto Niblick Road. From southbound Highway 101 take Pine Street, turn left onto 4th Street, left onto Spring Street, then left onto Niblick Road. From Niblick Road, turn right onto Country Club Drive.

This 6,215-yard, 18-hole, par-71 golf course offers public play, pro shop, restaurant, bar, lounge, banquet hall, reduced junior rates and incentives for frequent golfing. Carts available.

Paso Robles Municipal Pool

28th and Oak streets

(805) 237-3988

www.prcity.com/government/departments/recreation/aquatics/

$

From Highway 101 turn west onto 24th Street, right onto Spring Street, then left onto 28th Street.

The city's central pool facility offers one outdoor pool open through summer months and a smaller indoor pool open year round. The city offers various programs including swimming lessons, springboard diving lessons and water safety instruction. Call for current hours and offerings.

Pioneer Park

19th and Riverside Drive

(805) 237-3991

www.prcity.com/government/departments/recreation/facilities

FREE!

From southbound Highway 101 take the 16th Street exit, turn right onto Riverside Road. From northbound Highway 101 turn east onto 24th Street, then turn left onto Riverside Road.

This park comprises nearly 7 acres and includes a lighted softball field, a full basketball court, playground, restrooms, large barbecue area and Pioneer Skate Park.

Pioneer Skate Park

19th Ave at Riverside Drive (in Pioneer Park)

(805) 237-3991

www.prcity.com/government/departments/recreation/facilities

FREE!

From southbound Highway 101 take the 16th Street exit, turn right onto Riverside Road. From northbound Highway 101 turn east onto 24th Street, then turn left onto Riverside Road.

Helmets and pads are required at this free 10,500-square-foot concrete park that features a quarter pipe and rails.

The Ravine Water Park
2301 Airport Road
(805) 237-8500
www.ravinewaterpark.com
☛ $$

From Highway 101 take the Highway 46 exit and proceed east on Highway 46, then turn left onto Airport Road.

The north county's first large water park is slated to open in early 2007. The family-friendly 15-acre facility includes picnic areas, wave pool, 8,000-square-foot interactive kiddie pool, lazy river, two 250-foot-long flume water slides and two extreme water slides (a toilet bowl ride and a freefall slide). Other amenities include batting cages, go-kart track, food on site, private cabanas with wait service, volleyball courts, group picnic areas and banquet area.

The park is scheduled to be open from May to October from 10:30 a.m. to 8 p.m.

River Oaks Golf Course
700 Clubhouse Drive
(805) 226 - 2096
www.riveroaksgolfcourse.com
$

From Highway 101 take Highway 46 east, turn left onto North River Road, right onto River Oaks Drive and then left onto Clubhouse Drive.

This unique 6-hole golf course offers three sets of tees offering different angles of approach rather than simply extending distance to the greens. The course encourages family use with low rates and flexible play. The property also includes water features, a clubhouse and full-service restaurant.

Larry Moore Park
Riverbank Lane
(805) 237-3991
www.prcity.com/government/departments/recreation/facilities
FREE!

From southbound Highway 101 take the 4th Street/Pine St. exit, turn left onto 4th Street, left onto Spring Street, then left onto Niblick Road, then right onto South River Road and right onto Riverbank Lane. From northbound Highway 101 take the Spring Street exit, turn right onto Niblick Road, right onto South River Road and right onto Riverbank Lane.

This 21-acre open space includes plenty of running room, public restrooms and picnic tables. The completion of the River Parkways Project will add a 1½-mile riverside trail leading from the southern tip of the property, along the Salinas River north past the nearby shopping center.

Robbins Field
Park and 6th Street
(805) 237-3991
www.prcity.com/government/departments/recreation/facilities
FREE!

From southbound Highway 101 take the Pine Street exit and proceed north to the park. From northbound Highway 101 take the Spring Street exit and continue north, then turn right onto 6th Street.

This is a 2.4-acre ballpark that includes a lighted softball field with bleachers, announcer's booth and restrooms. It is regularly used for adult league, Little League and Junior Giant practices and games.

Royal Oak Meadows Park
Parkview Lane
(805) 237-3991
www.prcity.com/government/departments/recreation/facilities
FREE!

From Highway 101 northbound take Spring Street, turn right onto Niblick Road. From southbound Highway 101 take Paso Robles Street exit and proceed straight, turn right onto Creston Road, then left onto Niblick Road. Continue east on Niblick Road as it jogs and becomes Linne Road. Turn right onto Airport Road and right onto Parkview Lane.

This 2.4-acre park includes a playground, grass ball field with backstop and two small group barbecue areas.

Sherwood Park
At the corner of Scott Street and Creston Road
(805) 237-3991
www.prcity.com/government/departments/publicworks/
maintenance/little-league.asp
FREE!

From Highway 101 northbound take Spring Street, turn right onto Niblick Road, then right onto Creston Road. From southbound Highway 101 take Paso Robles Street exit and proceed straight, turn right onto Creston Road.

The 12.6 acre park is a focal point for the city's youth sports program. It includes a Little League field, softball field with bleachers, soccer fields, basketball court, sand volleyball court, four tennis courts and horseshoe pits. There are also group barbecue areas and restrooms.

Turtle Creek Park
Brookhill Drive
(805) 237-3991
www.prcity.com/government/departments/recreation/facilities

FREE!

From Highway 101 northbound take Spring Street, turn right onto Niblick Road. From southbound Highway 101 take Paso Robles Street exit and proceed straight, turn right onto Creston Road, then left onto Niblick Road. Continue east on Niblick Road as it jogs and becomes Linne Road. Turn right onto Airport Road, then right onto Brookhill Drive.

This 4.6-acre park includes a shuffle board, horseshoe pits, walking path, and four small barbecue areas.

OTHER ADVENTURES

Paso Bowl

2748 Spring St.

(805) 238-5020

$

From Highway 101 take the 24th Street exit and turn west onto 24th Street, then turn right onto Spring Street.

While other bowling alleys continue to fall off the map, this old favorite holds strong. Formerly known as Wilson's Lanes, the 16-lane Paso Bowl has been revamped. There is also a restaurant and cocktail lounge on site.

Paso Robles Children's Museum

623 13th Street

(805) 238-7432

www.pasokids.org

$

From northbound Highway 101 take Paso Robles Street north, then turn left onto 13th Street. From southbound Highway 101 take the 16th Street exit, turn left on Spring Street, then right onto 13th Street.

This museum-in-the-works will be located in the two-story firehouse on 13th Street.

Tobin James tasting room

8950 Union Road (off Highway 46)

(805) 239-2204

www.tobinjames.com

FREE!

From Highway 101 take Highway 46 east about 8 miles. Turn right onto Union Road.

Wine tasting is not traditionally a family affair, but Tobin James makes it possible at his rural tasting room. With a designated driver at the ready, adults can sip creative labels while kids enjoy the Old West theme of the tasting room (complete with 1860s-era mahogany bar from Blue Eye, Missouri), free arcade games and a bit of running room outside. The tasting

MISSION SAN MIGUEL ARCANGEL is among the many additional activities, sights and adventures to explore in the county's smaller communities and outlying areas.

Chapter 20

Outlying Areas & Day Trips

The outlying areas of San Luis Obispo County and extending into Santa Barbara and Monterey counties include plenty of spectacular scenery and family entertainment opportunities.

LETTERS

Creston Library
6290 Adams Street
Creston
(805) 237-3010
slolibrary.org/branch.htm
FREE!
From Highway 1 in Atascadero take Highway 41/Creston Eureka Road east. Turn right onto Highway 229/Webster Road, left onto Swayze Street, and then right onto Adams Street.
This branch of the San Luis Obispo County Library is open Mondays 2 p.m. to 7 p.m., and Tuesdays and Wednesdays from 1 p.m. to 6 p.m. Call for current schedule of activities.

Shandon Library
240 East Centre St.
Shandon
(805) 237-3009
slolibrary.org/branch.htm
FREE!
From Highway 101 take Highway 46 east, turn right onto McMillan Canyon Road/Highway 41 and proceed into Shandon.
This branch of the San Luis Obispo County Library is open Tuesdays and Thursdays from noon to 5 p.m. Call for current schedule of activities.

HISTORY

Camp Roberts Military Museum
Building 114, Camp Roberts
12 miles north of Paso Robles off Highway 101
(805) 238-3100
www.militarymuseum.org/CampRobertsMuseum.html

FREE!

Camp Roberts has served as a training center for the Army Reserve, National Guard and other military units since World War II. The museum boasts more than 3,000 items displayed in three buildings including the main museum, building 114 (Red Cross Headquarters) and Building 6585 (a World War II U.S. Post Office). Unusual features include exhibits on the Women's Army Corps, the WW II rail station, celebrities, and the hospital. The museum also includes a reference library, gift shop and large collection of vintage vehicles.

The museum is open Thursdays and Saturdays from 9 a.m. to 4 p.m. Tours are available by reservation.

Mission San Antonio de Padua

17 Mission Road
South of King City
(831) 385-4478
www.mchsmuseum.com/missionsant.html
FREE!

From Highway 101 take Jolon Road west to Mission Road.

This mission in southern Monterey County is unique among the 21 historic missions in that no city ever developed around it. The result is an opportunity to view the mission surrounded by wild California, much as it would have appeared more than 200 years ago. Look closely and you may still be able to spot portions of the aqueduct that brought water from the San Antonio River to the mission's grist mill, the first in California. Vandals have, unfortunately, damaged the original millstone and other historic elements, but the mission's setting remains one of the most authentic in the state.

The mission is open daily from 10 a.m. to 4 p.m. October through May, 8:30 a.m. to 6 p.m. June through September, and closed Christmas day. Mass is held here Sundays at 10 a.m.

Mission San Antonio de Padua, a National Historic Landmark and California Historic Place, is located on Fort Hunter Liggett Military Reservation, an active military training base. Base police aren't messing around when they enforce road closures, speed limits and other potential delays. Call ahead for current schedules, conditions and foreseeable delays.

Mission San Miguel Arcangel

Mission Street
San Miguel
(805) 467-2131
www.missionsanmiguel.org
☛ FREE!

From northbound Highway 101 take the Mission Street exit and proceed straight. From southbound Highway 101 take the 10th Street exit, turn left onto 10th Street, then right onto Mission Street.

The 16th of the California missions was heavily damaged in the 2003 San Simeon Earthquake, but its new designation as a National Historic Landmark may lead to the funding needed to repair the structure and eventual reopening.

Rios-Caledonia Adobe

700 S. Mission St.

San Miguel

(805) 467-3357

www.slocountyparks.com/facilities/rios_caledonia.htm

FREE!

From northbound Highway 101 take the Mission Street exit and proceed straight. From southbound Highway 101 take the 10th Street exit, turn left onto 10th Street, then right onto Mission Street.

RIOS-CALEDONIA ADOBE offers a window to the past.

The two-story adobe built in 1846 for Petronilo Rios is open Friday through Sunday from 11 a.m. to 4 p.m., though the grounds are open all daylight hours. The site includes restrooms, landscaped grounds with picnic benches, plentiful parking and a gift shop.

The structure originally served as the Rios family home. After change in ownership, the property was opened to the public as Caledonia Inn. It later served a variety of functions including home to various families, a mattress factory, a post office and a school.

NATURE

Big Sandy Wildlife Area

Indian Valley Road

San Miguel

(831) 649-7194

FREE!

From Highway 101 take the San Miguel/10th Street exit, turn east onto 10th street, left onto Mission Street, right onto River Road, then left onto Cross Canyons/Indian Valley Road, veering left as Indian Valley Road splits off.

Wild turkeys can often be spotted grazing, preening and impressing the hens in the county's wild places. Other predominant wildlife includes deer, foxes, coyotes, mountain lions, and the occasional bear.

This 850-acre wildlife area managed by the Department of Fish and Game is a designated hunting area. Archery equipment and shotguns are allowed here with hunting license. The area is also accessible to non-hunters. No camping is allowed, and since its primary purpose is to provide habitat for area wildlife, there are no maintained trails. Beware squirrel holes, rattle snakes, wild pigs and poison oak.

Big Sur
Highway 1 between San Simeon and Carmel
(831) 667-2100
www.bigsurcalifornia.org
Halfway between Santa Maria and San Francisco on world-famous Highway 1 is the rugged shoreline that served as inspiration for the likes of Jack Kerouac, Ansel Adams and just as likely your neighbor.

Ask friends, family, even random strangers to describe Big Sur and no two are likely to paint the same picture. One will reflect on family adventures building driftwood castles on the long stretch of sand at Andrew Molera State Park. Another will focus on the precipitous cliffs that separate Pacific Ocean from towering Santa Lucia mountain range. Some will recall heavy fog, dense shade, fresh incense of the forest. Others may reflect upon crashing waves, waterfalls and windswept beaches.

In fact, all these visitors are right on target when describing the 70-mile-long coastal region. The storied stretch of Highway 1 offers spectacular views of California's most rugged coastal area, a challenging road, the state's southernmost redwood forest, plentiful camping and hiking for all abilities.

The most daunting aspect of Big Sur is the drive.

Given a straight, well-maintained, wide road, the drive up the coast would take only a few short hours. In reality, the winding trip up winding Highway 1 slows, often to jogging pace, just north of San Simeon. Hairpin turns and treacherous cliffs slow even the most aggressive drivers. Lumbering motorhomes and gutsy bicyclists slow the rest of us.

Thanks in no small part to this challenging access, the area has gone largely unchanged since Juan Cabrillo first noted it in 1542. While trails metamorphosed into roads crisscrossing the state for the following three and a half centuries, access to Big Sur was limited to trails. It wasn't until 1937 that a treacherous wagon trail from Carmel to Big Sur was improved and extended to become today's well-traveled route through to San Simeon.

Once there, expect no strip malls, no big box stores, not even a large grocery store in Big Sur.

There is, however, plenty of room for tents, backpacks, hiking boots, children and those seeking to commune with nature. There are thick forests of fragrant redwoods and Monterey pine, miles upon miles of mountainous hiking trails, blufftop trails and beachcombing opportunity galore.

Parks include: Andrew Molera State Park, featuring an easy 1-mile hike to the driftwood-laden beach; Pfeiffer Big Sur State Park with riverside and redwood camping, hiking trails directly out of the campground into redwood forests and to the Pfeiffer Falls; Julia Pfeiffer Burns State Park with its famous view of McWay Falls.

Winter weather can create landslides that close Highway 1 fairly regularly. Beware of poison oak which grows abundantly along the coastal region and keep an eye out for traffic. Pull over at any of a number of scenic turnouts to let faster vehicles pass while you safely take in the view.

C.W. Clarke Park
First Street
Shandon
(805) 781-5200
www.slocountyparks.com
FREE!
From Highway 101 take Highway 46 east, turn right onto McMillan Canyon Road/Highway 41 and proceed into Shandon.

This 11-acre park houses the county parks department's largest public pool. Though the pool is open summers only, the remainder of the parks facilities are open year round including basketball courts, tennis courts, and football and baseball fields. A park host is also available.

Guadalupe-Nipomo Dunes Preserve
West Main Street
Guadalupe in Santa Barbara County
(805) 343-9151
www.fws.gov/hoppermountain/Guadalupe
www.dunescenter.org
FREE!
From Highway 101 in Santa Maria take Main Street/Highway 166 West through town, and fields before arriving at its end at the beach.

The GUADALUPE-NIPOMO DUNES COMPLEX offers miles of sand and shore.

This 18-mile stretch of coastline, dunes and estuaries offers seemingly endless walks, wildlife viewing opportunities and plenty of sand for castles. Whales are often spotted from this stretch of coastline that is also home to endangered California least tern and California red-legged frog, and the threatened Western snowy plover. The area is also home to the Guadalupe-Nipomo Dunes National Wildlife Refuge.

Though the waves may be inviting, this is not an ideal place to enter the Pacific. Riptides abound here, the waves can be enormous and the sandy edge quickly drops to a deep shelf. Children should be attended closely. Wading is discouraged since sweeper waves occur regularly here.

The non-profit Guadalupe Dunes Center in nearby Guadalupe (1055 Guadalupe St., 805-343-2455) offers docent-led walks and other educational programs throughout the year.

The Nature Conservancy controls the southernmost access to the complex and encourages donations at the entrance kiosk, but there is no mandatory fee.

Nacimiento Lake
10625 Nacimiento Lake Drive
Paso Robles
(805) 238-3256
www.nacimientoresort.com
$$

From Highway 101 take the 24th Street exit and proceed west through town. Follow Nacimiento Lake Drive to the right as it splits off from 24th Street.

Generations of Central Coast families have spent countless weekends, holidays and lazy summer afternoons along the shore of this man-made lake. With 167 miles of shoreline and 5,370 surface acres of water there's usually enough room for waterskiing and fishing, camping and hiking. The marina offers boat and jet ski rentals. Nearby Nacimiento Resort offers a restaurant, groceries, fuel, bait, tackle and other supplies.

Parkfield
Cholame Valley Road
(805) 463-2421
www.Parkfield.com
FREE!

From Highway 101 turn east onto Highway 46 and continue out of town, past Shandon and through Cholame. Turn left onto Cholame Valley Road just a couple hundred feet before the Highway 41/Highway 46 split.

This tiny rural community on the San Andreas Fault has been made famous by its relatively regular significant earthquakes. As a result, it was selected by the U.S. Geological Survey for a comprehensive, long-term earthquake research project aptly named The Parkfield Experiment.

The area also offers spectacular shows of wildflowers in the spring, an annual bluegrass festival held every Mother's Day weekend and an annual rodeo.

Pinnacles National Monument
East of Soledad in Monterey County
(831) 389-4485
www.nps.gov/pinn
$

East entrance: From Highway 101 at King City take Bitterwater Road north to Highway 25. Turn left and continue, following signs to the entrance.

West entrance: From Highway 101 at Soledad, take the Front Street/El Camino Real exit, turn east onto Highway 146 and follow the signs to the park.

The dark recesses of Balconies Caves offer an ants-eye view of the world. Gigantic boulders are wedged precariously in the cracked cliffs overhead like the gravel and sand that form the delicately balanced anthill. For some, the caves are the high point of Pinnacles National Monument. Other favorites include technical rock climbing opportunities, the park's 30 miles of trails, and more than 160 species of birds.

Formation of the namesake peaks began millions of years ago inside the heart of a volcano. Erosion, plate tectonics and faulting have washed the volcano's shell away, some of it as far south as the Los Angeles basin. The remaining spires are best viewed from the park's west entrance or along the steep and strenuous High Peaks Trail. There are no roads connecting the two park entrances, so visitors interested in both angles must either drive the long way around or plan to spend some time on the foot trails that link the two entrances.

This 24,200-acre park set aside in 1908 as a natural preserve and recreation area offers plentiful opportunity for hands-on lessons in geology, botany, wildlife and outdoor survival. The nearest campground is a half mile east of the eastern gate. The privately operated camp includes flush toilets, pay showers, a pool and well-stocked little store. Raccoons and wild boars sometimes plague campers. We learned that raccoons, just like cats, will climb atop cars to reach their booty. The sites were well spaced, though sound traveled clearly from one fire ring to the next. Morning wakeup calls included the tunes of magpies, bluejays, Stellar jays, quail, hawks, doves, owls, woodpeckers, towhees, hummingbirds, junkos, woodpeckers.

The store clerk said the park is usually busiest in spring months as wildflowers spread their petals and temperatures are at their best. During summer months, trailside temperatures can often reach 100 degrees.

Old Pinnacles Trail is a good place for families to start. Wildflowers along the route include Sticky Monkeyflower, Indian Paintbrush, Wooly Blue Curls, California Poppy, Miner's Lettuce and Fiddleneck. The trail starts easy enough, but gives way to a more moderate stretch just over two quiet miles from the trailhead at Chalone Creek Picnic Area. As we rounded a corner, we suddenly faced a wall of rock. A clearly marked trail led us into the talus cave where the going got pretty rough, but much more entertaining. A flashlight is a must for anyone interested in passing completely through the half-mile natural tunnel. At points, hikers are completely enveloped in blackness. Finding the way without a light may not be impossible, but certainly would be dangerous.

We climbed up and over, sidled through, squeezed between and, at times, crawled under boulders varying in size from small treasure chests to large homes. And just as quickly as we had come upon the caves we were out of them. In the narrow canyon above, we found a fantastically cool spot to rest our packs, enjoy lunch and take a close look at the rocks and plants.

For those seeking direction, park rangers lead nature hikes every Saturday and Sunday through May. The hikes begin at 10 a.m. from the Bear Gulch Visitor Center on the east side of the park and at 2 p.m. from the Chaparral Ranger Station on the west. The park also offers interpretive talks, night hikes, and bat education programs.

No dogs on any trails, though they are allowed in parking and picnic areas. The park is open 7:30 a.m. to 8 p.m. daily. No overnight camping inside the park boundary. Bear Gulch Cave closed indefinitely. Watch out for poison oak, rattlesnakes and heat.

Point Sal State Beach

Point Sal Road
Near Guadalupe in Santa Barbara County
(800) 777-0369

www.parks.ca.gov/?page_id=605

☛ FREE!

From Highway 101 take Main Street exit in Santa Maria and head west. Turn left onto Ray Road, then right onto Brown Road. Continue west on Brown Road across Highway 1 then follow the road as it curves toward the locked gate at the bottom of Point Sal Road.

While the Bureau of Land Management does not provide public access to its 77-acre Point Sal promontory, state parks does allow cyclists and hikers to access Point Sal Beach south of the point. The 9-mile roundtrip isn't for the faint of heart, whether traveled on foot or on pedals.

The road that once provided public access to this beautiful stretch of white sand was wiped out by winter storms in the 1990s and the powers that were opted not to restore the road. While many portions of the road remain in decent repair, complete sections have been wiped out. There only single-track trails remain.

Only experienced cyclists should make any portion of this trip as it involves a long, unrelenting climb/descent. But the graded dirt road, sections of pavement and even the single-track that leads down toward the beach are clearly well traveled.

The joy in this journey doesn't require reaching the beach. Adventurers who reach the ridge are rewarded with expansive views often accompanied by the sounds of waves and sea lions from the beach below.

SAN ANTONIO LAKE offers 60 miles of shoreline sprinkled with wildflowers and sprawling oaks.

San Antonio Lake
Nacimiento Lake Road
Paso Robles
(805) 472-2311
$$

From Highway 101 take the 24th Street exit and proceed west through town. Follow Nacimiento Lake Drive to the right as it splits off from 24th Street. Continue past Nacimiento Lake and past Interlake Road to San Antonio Lake.

Like Nacimiento Lake, its neighbor to the south, San Antonio Lake serves up plenty of fishing, waterskiing and general family fun. The man-made lake boasts 5,500 surface acres of water and 60 miles of shoreline. Boat rentals are offered at the marina, and shoreline camping is plentiful.

San Miguel Park

1221 K Street

(805) 781-5200

www.slocountyparks.com

From Highway 101 take the 10th Street exit, turn east onto 10th Street, then left onto K Street.

This park is located on the site of a school dating back to the 1800s. Today it includes a skinned ball field, playground and restrooms. It is also home to the community pool that is open summer months only.

Resources & Indexes

Resources

Books

Some things are better left alone. For a complete rundown on the great outdoors, check out these books, most of which are available at local bookstores including Novel Experience, 779 Higuera St., and Mountain Air Sports, 667 Marsh St. Suite D, both in San Luis Obispo.

San Luis Obispo County Trail Guide, by Santa Lucia Chapter, Sierra Club
Day Hikes San Luis Obispo County California, by Robert Stone
Mountain Biking the Central Coast, by Carol Berlund

Chambers of Commerce

These business associations promote their communities with an emphasis on membership. While these are great places to start your search for local information, keep in mind that most fail to mention non-member businesses, so their information isn't always all inclusive.

Arroyo Grande Chamber of Commerce
800 West Branch St.
Arroyo Grande, CA 93420
(805) 489-1488
www.arroyograndecc.com

Atascadero Chamber of Commerce
6550 El Camino Real
Atascadero, CA 93422-4202
(805) 466-2044
www.atascaderochamber.org

Cambria Chamber of Commerce
767 Main St.
Cambria, CA 93428
(805) 927-3624
www.cambriachamber.org

Cayucos Chamber of Commerce
158 N. Ocean Ave.
Cayucos, CA 93430
(805) 995-1200
www.cayucoschamber.com

Grover Beach Chamber
180 Highway 1
Grover Beach, CA 93433
(805) 489-9091
www.groverchamber.com

Los Osos/Baywood Park Chamber of Commerce
781 Palisades Ave.
P.O. Box 6282
Los Osos, CA 93412

(805) 528-4884
www.losososbaywoodpark.org/chamber
Morro Bay Chamber of Commerce
845 Embarcadero, #D
Morro Bay, CA 93442-2147
(805) 772-4467
www.morrobay.org
Nipomo Chamber of Commerce
671 West Tefft St., Ste 8
Nipomo, CA 93444-8988
(805) 929-1583
www.nipomochamber.org
Paso Robles Chamber of Commerce
1225 Park Street
Paso Robles, CA 93446
(805) 238-0506
www.pasorobleschamber.com
Pismo Beach Chamber of Commerce
581 Dolliver St.
Pismo Beach, CA 93449
(805) 773-4382
www.pismochamber.com
San Luis Obispo Chamber of Commerce
1039 Chorro St.
San Luis Obispo, CA 93401
(805) 781-2777
www.slochamber.org
Templeton Chamber of Commerce
P.O. Box 701
Templeton, CA 93465
(805) 434-1789
San Luis Obispo County Visitors & Conference Bureau
811 El Capitan Way, #200
San Luis Obispo, CA 93401
(805) 541-8000
www.SanLuisObispoCounty.com
Central Coast Agritourism Council
545 Main St., B-1
Morro Bay, CA 93442
(800) 918-1999
www.agadventures.org

Recreation and Parks Departments

These governmental departments provide activities and amenities for all ages.
Atascadero Parks & Recreation Department (805) 461-5000
Arroyo Grande Parks & Recreation Department (805)
Cambria Parks & Recreation Department (805) 927-7776
Grover Beach Parks & Recreation Department (805) 473-4580

Morro Bay Recreation & Parks Department (805) 772-6278
Nipomo Area Recreation Association (805) 929-5437
Paso Robles Recreation Division (805) 237-3991
Pismo Beach Recreation Division (805) 773-7063
San Luis Obispo Parks & Recreation Department (805) 781-7283
Templeton Parks Department (805) 434-4900
San Luis Obispo County Parks (805) 781-5930

Farmers' Markets

On any given day you can find some sort of farmers' market going on in
San Luis Obispo County. They are organized by a variety of associations,
and all include produce from local (and sometimes not-so-local) farms.

Many of the markets also include crafts, games and live entertainment.

The following list of locations and times is subject to change. Check local
newspaper listings or chambers of commerce for the latest information or
check in with organizers.

Arroyo Grande
(805) 544-9570
www.slocountyfarmers.org
Saturday, 9 a.m. to 11:30 a.m. in the Village behind City Hall
Wednesday, 9:00 to 11:30 a.m., Arroyo Grande at K-Mart on Oak Park Road
Saturday, Noon to 2:30 p.m. at City Hall Parking Lot off East Branch Street

Atascadero
(805) 466-2044
www.countryfarmandcraftmarket.com/market.html
Seasonal – Wednesday, 3:00 p.m.-6:00 p.m., East Mall, El Camino Real
(Palma and Entrada)
Wednesdays, 6 p.m. to 8 p.m., 7500 block El Camino Real

Avila Beach
www.visitavilabeach.com
April through October, Friday, 4 p.m. to 8 p.m., Front Street Plaza

Cambria
(805) 927-3624
www.cambriachamber.org/
Friday, 2:30 – 5:30 p.m., Veterans Hall parking lot, 1000 Main St.

Cayucos
(805) 995-1200
www.cayucoschamber.com/#Events
April through November, Friday, 9:30 to 11:30 a.m., Cayucos Veteran's
Hall, 10 Cayucos Dr.

Los Osos/Baywood Park
(805) 239-6535
losososbaywoodpark.org
Monday, 2 p.m. to 4:30 p.m., Santa Maria Avenue between 2nd and 3rd Streets

Morro Bay
(805) 544-9570
www.slocountyfarmers.org

Thursday Fishermen's and Farmers' Market, 3 p.m. to 5 p.m., Spencer's Market, 2650 Main St.
Saturday, 4 p.m. to 7 p.m., 800 block Main St.
Nipomo
 (805) 929-3081
www.mynipomo.com
Sundays ,11:30 a.m. to 2:30 p.m., 671 W. Tefft St.
Paso Robles
(805) 237-9254
www.countryfarmandcraftmarket.com/market.html
Tuesday, 4 p.m. to 7 p.m., City Park, 11th and Spring St.
Friday, 9 a.m. to 12:30 p.m., 180 Niblick Road
Saturday, 8 a.m. to noon, City Park, 11th and Spring Streets
San Luis Obispo
(805) 544-9570
www.slocountyfarmers.org/
Thursday, 6 p.m. to 9 p.m., Higuera Street from Osos Street to Nipomo Street
Saturday, 8 a.m. to 10:30 a.m., Madonna Shopping Center, Madonna Road
San Miguel
www.discoversanmiguel.com/market.html
San Miguel Country Farm & Craft Market
Seasonal, Sundays, 10 a.m. to 2 p.m., Mission and 10th streets
Templeton
(805) 239-6535
www.templetonchamber.com
Saturday, 9 a.m. to noon, 6th and Crocker streets

Arts Associations
Allied Arts Association Schoolhouse Gallery
    P.O. Box 184, Cambria, CA 93428   (805) 927-8190
    www.artistsofcambria.com
Atascadero Art Association
    P.O. Box 28, Atascadero, CA 93423   (805) 462-0632
    www.atascaderoartassn.fix.net
Cal Poly Arts
    1 Grand Ave., San Luis Obispo, CA 93407   (805) 756-7110
    www.calpolyarts.org
Cayucos Art Association
    (805) 995-2049
    www.cayucos.org/caa
Cayucos Mural Society
    97 10th St. #3, Cayucos, CA 93430   (805) 995-3539
    www.cayucos.org/muralsociety
Children's Creative Project
    520 Bernardo Ave., Morro Bay, CA 93442   (805) 772-0656
Paso Robles Art Association
    1315 Vine St., Paso Robles, CA 93446   (805) 238-5473

San Luis Obispo Art Center
1010 Broad St., San Luis Obispo, CA 93401   (805) 543-8562
www.sloartcenter.org
San Luis Obispo County Arts Council
P.O. Box 1710, San Luis Obispo, CA 93406   (805) 544-9251
www.sloartscouncil.org

Music Associations
Mozart Festival Association
P.O. Box 311, San Luis Obispo, CA 93406   (805) 781-3008
www.mozartfestival.com
Music and Arts for Youth
P.O. Box 13752, San Luis Obispo, CA 93406   (805) 541-4456
Pacific Repertory Opera
P.O. Box 14760, San Luis Obispo, CA 93406   (805) 541-5369
www.propera.org
San Luis Obispo Blues Society
P.O. Box 14041, San Luis Obispo, CA 93406   (805) 541-7930
home.kcbx.net/~sloblues/
San Luis Obispo County Youth Symphony
P.O. Box 430, San Luis Obispo, CA 93406   (805) 546-8742
www.sloyouthsymphony.org
San Luis Obispo Folk Music Society
2465 Tierra Drive, Los Osos, CA 93402   (805) 528-8963
www.slofolks.org
San Luis Obispo Symphony
P.O. Box 658, San Luis Obispo, CA 93406   (805) 546-8742
www.slosymphony.com
San Luis Obispo Vocal Arts Ensemble
P.O. Box 4306, San Luis Obispo, CA 93406   (805) 541-6797
www.vocalarts.org
SLO Jazz Federation
P.O. Box 1888, Morro Bay, CA 93443   (805) 546-3733
www.slojazz.org

Theatrical Organizations
Cal Poly Theatre and Dance
1 Grand Ave., San Luis Obispo, CA 93407   (805) 756-1248
cla.calpoly.edu/thtrdanc
Central Coast Shakespeare Festival
P.O. Box 175, San Luis Obispo, CA 93406   (805) 546-4224
www.ccshakes.org
Civic Ballet of San Luis Obispo
672 Higuera St., San Luis Obispo, CA 93401   (805) 544-4363
civicballetofslo.org
Clark Center for the Performing Arts
487 Fair Oaks Ave., Arroyo Grande, CA 93420   (805) 489-9444
www.clarkcenter.org

Corners of the Mouth Poetry Festival
393 D Buchon St., San Luis Obispo, CA 93401(805) 547-1318
www.languageofthesoul.org

Cuesta College Performing Arts
Cuesta College, Hwy. 1, SLO, CA 93401   (805) 546-3100
academic.cuesta.edu/performingarts

Foundation for the Performing Arts Center
P.O. Box 1137, San Luis Obispo, CA 93406   (805) 541-5401
www.pacslo.org/events

The Great American Melodrama & Vaudeville Revue
1863 Pacific Blvd., Oceano, CA 93475   (805) 489-2499

Interact Theatre
Cuesta College, Hwy. 1, SLO, CA 93401   (805) 546-3282

Pewter Plough Playhouse
P.O. Box 494., Cambria, CA 93428   (805) 927-3877
www.pewterploughplayhouse.org

Pioneer Players
1339 Riverside Ave., Paso Robles, CA 93446   (805) 239-1638

San Luis Obispo High School Theater
1499 San Luis Dr., San Luis Obispo, CA 93401(805) 596-4040

San Luis Obispo Little Theatre
888 Morro St., San Luis Obispo, CA 93406   (805) 786-2440

Public Transit

The county is full of public transportation options, though some are more convenient than others. Many of the area's buses include bike racks. All require exact change, and any transfers needed should be requested upon boarding. See each city for local listings. The following are offered countywide.

Regional Transit Authority (RTA)
(805) 541-2228
www.slorta.org
Countywide bus system includes most cities in the county, plus Cal Poly, Cuesta College, Hearst Castle and Santa Maria in neighboring Santa Barbara County.

Regional Transit Authority/South County Transit (SCAT)
(805) 541-2228
www.cattransit.org
Bus routes specific to southern San Luis Obispo County including Arroyo Grande, Grover Beach, Oceano, Pismo Beach, Shell Beach. The service also runs the Avila Beach Trolley.

SLO Transit
This public bus service canvases the city and operates the Downtown Trolley.
(805) 541-BUS (541-2877)
www.ridshare.org/buses/slotransit.htm

Paso Robles City Area Transit Service (PRCATS)
(805) 239-8747

www.ridshare.org/buses/prsched.htm

This bus service serves the city from 7 a.m. to 7 p.m. Monday through Saturday except holidays.

Atascadero Transit/El Camino Shuttle
(805) 466-7433

www.rideshare.org/buses/atassched.htm

This service runs from 7 a.m. to 7 p.m. Mondays through Saturdays throughout the year except holidays. Serves Atascadero and runs a shuttle to Templeton.

Cambria Village Trolley
(805) 781-4472

Free summertime transportation linking Cambria Village businesses and Highway 1 is also available Fridays through Sundays the rest of the year.

Morro Bay Trolley
(805) 772-6200

For 25 cents, adults can grab a ride along either of two routes through summer months. Weekend service continues into October. Children under 40 inches tall ride free.

Ride-On
(805) 541-TRIP (541-8747)

www.ride-on.org

This non-profit organization promotes community transportation through ridesharing, busing and shuttle services. It provides airport shuttles, lunchtime express shuttle service and carpooling information as well as current information about all area public transportation options.

Runabout
(805) 541-2544

All vehicles on this shuttle service are wheelchair equipped and available Monday through Saturday countywide, and daily in San Luis Obispo.

Senior Shuttle
(805) 541-8747

Ride-On Transportation provides low-cost senior transportation by reservation. South County service is available Tuesdays and Thursdays. North County service is available Wednesdays, and North Coast service is on Mondays.

Clubs, Groups and Other Gatherings

A Pound of Pianists
(805) 474-9474
Piano players meet in the South County.

Almond Country Quilters Guild
www.almondcountryquilters.org
Trinity Lutheran Church
940 Creston Road
Paso Robles
Meets 6:30 p.m. the first Monday of each month.

Amateur Radio Club
(805) 226-9990
Centennial Park
600 Nickerson Drive
Paso Robles
Meets at 7:30 p.m. the first Monday of each month.

Arroyo Grande Community Chorus
(805) 489-1486
Room 150, Arroyo Grande High School
495 Valley Road
Arroyo Grande
Singers high school aged and older are invited to sing together at 6:30 p.m. Tuesdays throughout the school year.

Attachment Parenting Support Group
(805) 462-1962
"Kangaroo Club" meets weekly throughout the county.

Atascadero Horesemen's Club
(805) 466-2699
Meets at Players Restaurant
8845 El Camino Real
Atascadero
Meets at 7 p.m. on the second Tuesday of each month to plan and discuss rides, projects and other club events.

Atascadero Native Tree Association
(805) 461-7610
Meets at Ranger House
Atascadero Lake Park
Meets at 5:30 p.m. the second Monday of each month.

Bear Valley Quilters
(805) 528-2183
Meets at South Bay Community Center

2180 Palisades Ave.
Meets at 6:30 p.m. the fourth Monday of each month.

The Bead Society Club
(805) 238-3797
Howe's Beads & Crafts
840 13th St.
Paso Robles
Meets at 10 a.m. on the third Saturday of each month

Boy Scouts of America
(805) 543-5766
Call for local troop information.

California Dressage Society, SLO Chapter
(805) 438-3543
Meeting times and locations vary.

Cambria Computer Club
(805) 927-8844
Meets at Joslyn Recreation Center
950 Main St.
Cambria
Meets at 2 p.m. the first three Thursdays of the month.

Central Coast Baton Twirling Club
(805) 245-0245
Meets at 4:30 p.m. the last Friday of each month on the fourth floor of
Atascadero City Hall, 6500 Palma Ave.

Central Coast Art Doll Club
(805) 528-3758
Meets 10 a.m. to 12:30 p.m. on the third Monday of each month at The
Cottonball Classroom, 475 Morro Bay Blvd., Morro Bay.

Central Coast Classy Birds Car Club
(805) 772-3224
This club is for owners of 1955-57 Thunderbirds. Call for meeting times
and locations.

Central Coast Follies
(80t) 543-9452
Singers and dancers of all ages gather Wednesdays from 11:15 a.m. to 1:15
a.m. for performances at Moose Hall, 180 Main St., Pismo Beach.

Central Coast Geological Society
(805) 438-3876

Meets at 6:30 p.m. on the second Thursday of each month at A.J. Spurs Restaurant, 777 N. Oak Park Blvd., Grover Beach.

Central Coast Mothers of Multiples
(805) 239-4898
Regular meetings and playdates designed specifically for mothers of twins, triplets and more.

Central Coast Natural History Association
(805) 772-2694 x101
Through the efforts of its members, the association supports educational and conservation works throughout state parks located on the Central Coast.

Central Coast Quilters
(805) 489-9786
Meets at 6:30 p.m. the fourth Tuesday of each month at Arroyo Grande Community Center, 211 Vernon Ave., Arroyo Grande

Central Coast Scottish Society and Pipe & Drum Band
(805) 771-9900
Meets from 7 p.m. to 9 p.m. the third Thursday of each month at Dairy Creek Golf Course, Highway 1 north of San Luis Obispo.

Central Coast Treasure Hunters Association
(805) 489-1592
This club of metal-detection enthusiasts, featured in Life Magazine, meets at 7:30 p.m. the fourth Thursday of each month at the County Board of Education Office, 3350 Education Drive off Highway 1 north of Cuesta College.

Central Coast Water Polo Club
www.ccwp.us

Central Coast Weavers Guild
(805) 474-6889
Meets the second Thursday of each month.

Central Coast Woodcarvers
(805) 927-5240
Meets from 10 a.m. to 3 p.m. Wednesdays at the Cayucos Veterans Memorial Building, 201 Ocean Front Ave., Cayucos.

Central Coast Woodturners
(805) 929-1423
Members meet at 9 a.m. on the third Saturday of each month to talk about current projects, show their work, see guest presenters and introduce a new challenge project each month. Amateurs to pros alike are invited.

Cuesta Guitar Circle
(805) 474-9444
Classical guitarists meet at 7 p.m. on the third Thursday of each month at the Conference Center, room 5402, Cuesta College, Highway 1, San Luis Obispo.

Donut Derelicts of Pismo Beach
(805) 473-5801
Car enthusiasts of all sorts, particularly sports cars, antiques, collector cars and hot rods, meet at 8 a.m. Saturdays in the shopping center parking lot at Oak Park Road and James Way.

Embroiderers' Guild of America, Bishop's Peak
(805) 473-9268
Meets from 10 a.m. to 1 p.m. the third Saturday of each month at Grover Beach Community Center, 1230 Trouville Ave., Grover Beach

Estero Radio Club
(805) 528-8900
www.sloradio.net
Amateur radio operators meets at 1 p.m. the second Saturday of each month at the Sherriff's Department auditorium, 1585 Kansas Ave., San Luis Obispo.

Estrella Warbird Museum
(805) 227-0440
Learn about aeronautical war machines, or help renovate some. The organization holds a monthly dinner meeting at Glen Thompson Hall, 4251 A Dry Creek Road, Paso Robles Airport, Paso Robles.

Families with Children from China
(805) 544-4075
Monthly meetings, play dates and support group for those who have, are waiting for or considering adopting children from China.

For Youth's Interest (FYI)
(805) 461-5000 x3472
City-organized youth group for Atascadero area teens interested in building positive friendships and leadership skills.

Friends of the Adobes
(805) 467-3357
Regular meetings and projects organized in the best interest of the area's historic adobe structures.

Gem and Mineral Club
(805) 772-7260

Meets at 7 p.m. the first Tuesday of each month at SLO Senior Citizens Center, 1455 Santa Rosa St., San Luis Obispo.

German-American Club of the Central Coast
(805) 462-0717
Meets at 7 p.m. the second Wednesday of each month. Call for current location.

Girl Scouts, Tres Condados Council
(800)822-2427
Call for local troop information.

Granola
(805) 783-1392
Parent-child group meets every Wednesday at 10:30 a.m. to discuss community, home schooling and family fun.

Hiking Moms
(805) 541-4221
Hikes held the first and third Tuesday of each month at 10 a.m. Bring child, carrier, diapers, snacks and plenty of water.

Inventors and Entrepreneurs Workshop, SLO Chapter
(805) 549-0401
Meets at 6:30 p.m. the last Thursday of each month at the Cuesta College Small Business Development Center, 3566 S. Higuera St., Suite 100, San Luis Obispo.

Italian-Speaking Group
(805) 922-6966 x3422
Meets from 2 p.m. to 4 p.m. the second and fourth Saturdays of each month at Linnaea's Café, 1110 Garden St., San Luis Obispo.

Knitters' Guild
(805) 781-8881
Meets from 10 a.m. to noon the second and fourth Saturdays of each month at SLO City/County Library, 995 Palm St., San Luis Obispo.

La Leche League International
(805) 489-9128
This breastfeeding support organization meets regularly.

Mid-State Cruizers Classic Car Club
(805) 466-3853
Meets at 6 p.m. the third Thursday of each month at Player's Restaurant, 8845 El Camino Real, Atascadero.

Momma Bears of SLO County
(805) 801-7218
Meets weekly for support and playgroups.

Moms Club of Atascadero
(805) 438-3531
Meets from 10:30 a.m. to 2 p.m. Thursdays and for playgroups, support, activities at various locations.

Moms Club of Paso Robles
(805) 239-0291
Meets weekly for playgroups, support, activities at various locations.

Moms Club of SLO
(805) 595-1452
This support group for mothers meets regularly for activities, field trips, mom's night out and includes a babysitting cooperative. Call for current schedule of activities and locations.

Moms Club of South SLO County
(805) 489-6569
This support group for mothers meets monthly and plans various activities throughout the year. Call for current schedule.

Morro Coast Audubon Society
(805) 528-8193
Meets at 7:30 p.m. on the third Monday of months September through June at Congregational Church, 11245 Los Osos Valley Road, San Luis Obispo.

Muddy Bog Juggling Club
(805) 772-2759
Meets from 6:30 p.m. to 8:30 p.m. Tuesdays in the cafeteria at Cuesta College and from 5 p.m. to 7 p.m. Thursdays at Cal Poly's student government room.

National Association of Watch and Clock Collectors
(805) 528-3100
Meets 12:30 p.m. second Sundays at Senior Center Hall, 1580 Railroad St., Oceano.

Newborn and Older Class
(805) 543-6988
Mothers and fathers alike are welcome to these free weekly classes to discuss feeding, crying and sleep (or lack thereof).

North County Aquatics
P.O. Box 1933

Paso Robles, CA 93447

(805) 239-3013

www.northcountyaquatics.org

A USA Swimming-affiliated competitive swim team serving residents of northern San Luis Obispo County. Swimmers of all abilities ages 5 to 18 are eligible for the program.

Olde Towne Quilters of Nipomo

(805) 929-3704

Two meetings held the fourth Thursday of each month. The 10 a.m. meeting, held at St. Joseph's Church, 298 S. Thompson Ave., includes trunk shows, guest speakers and other presentations. The guild meets again at 6:30 p.m. for a friendship gathering.

Pacific Horizon Chorus

(805) 528-6106

Female voices interested in singing in four-part harmony are invited to join this member of Sweet Adelines International, a society that supports the preservation of barbershop style choral singing. The chorus practices every Tuesday from 7 p.m. to 9:30 p.m. at San Luis Coastal Adult School, 1500 Lizzie St., Room J4, San Luis Obispo.

Pinochle

(805) 481-7886

Learn to play or bring your prowess at 12:30 p.m. Tuesdays, Central Coast Senior Center, 1580 Railroad St., Oceano.

Pismo Beach Walking Club

(805) 489-9777

Meets south of Pismo Pier at 7:25 a.m. Mondays, Wednesdays and Fridays.

Puma Aquatics

(805) 704-2370

www.pumaswim.org/home.htm

This USA Swimming-affiliated competitive swim team practices in Atascadero and at Cuesta College near San Luis Obispo. Swimmers of all abilities ages 5 to 18 are eligible for the program.

Ride Nipomo

(805) 343-9494

Meets regularly for horse-related events and meetings. Call for current schedule.

San Luis Obispo County 4-H

(805) 781-5943

4-H is a co-educational youth development program overseen by the University of California Cooperative Extension. The learn-by-doing program is designed for youth in grades 4 and up, though primary members as young as 5 years old may be allowed. Projects range from citizenship and leadership to science and technology.

San Luis Obispo Rugby Football Club
(805) 786-6860
A seriously competitive rugby club for the rough-and-tumble kids at heart.

San Luis Obispo Swim Club (aka San Luis Obispo Seahawks)
P.O. Box 142
San Luis Obispo, CA 93406
(805) 543-9515
www.sloseahawks.org
A USA Swimming-affiliated competitive swim team serving San Luis Obispo and surrounding areas. Swimmers of all abilities ages 5 to 18 are eligible for the program.

SLO Bicycle Club
(805) 543-5973
Avid cyclists, primarily road riders, meet at 7 p.m. the first Thursday of each month at the SLO Senior Citizens Center, 1445 Santa Rosa St., San Luis Obispo.

SLO Bytes PC Users Group
www.slobytes.org
Meets from 1 p.m. to 4:30 p.m. the first Sunday of each month at Odd Fellows Hall, 520 Dana St., San Luis Obispo.

SLO Chess Club
(805) 544-0717
All ages and levels are invited for the Thursday meetings from 6:30 p.m. to 10 p.m. All equipment is provided in the craft room, Church of the Nazarene, 3396 Johnson Ave., San Luis Obispo.

SLO County Four Wheel Drive Club
www.slo4wheelers.org
Meets at 7 p.m. on the first Wednesday of each month at Player's Restaurant, 8845 El Camino Real, Atascadero

SLO County Genealogical Society
(805) 473-4963
Meets at 12:30 p.m. the first Saturdays except July, August and December at Odd Fellows Hall, 520 Dana St., San Luis Obispo.

SLO Camera Club
(805) 786-0710
Meets at 7:30 p.m the fourth Tuesday of each month at 6588 Ontario Road, San Luis Obispo.

SLO Muzzleloaders
(805) 528-6426
Meets at 9 a.m. second Sundays at SLO Sportsmen's Association, 3272 Gilardi Road.

SLO Philatelic Society
(805) 547-9022
Stamp collectors meet at 1 p.m. the first Tuesday and 7 p.m. the third Thursday of each month at Church of Christ fellowship hall, 3172 Johnson Ave., San Luis Obispo.

SLO Quilters
(805) 544-4218
Meets at 7 p.m. second Mondays at Congregational United Church of Christ, 11245 Los Osos Valley Road, San Luis Obispo.

SLO Rowing Club
(805) 466-9507
Meets at 8 a.m. Saturdays and Sundays, 7 a.m. Thursdays at Santa Margarita Lake.

SLO Skiers
(805) 549-7777
Meets at 7:30 p.m. first and third Thursdays year round at Embassy Suites Hotel, 333 Madonna Road, San Luis Obispo.

SLO Vettes Car Club
(805) 434-2724
Corvette owners meet at 6 p.m. second Fridays alternating between Atascadero and San Luis Obispo. Call for current schedule.

Santa Lucia Flyfishers
(805) 489-7416
Meets the second Thursday of each month at 6 p.m. at Margie's Diner, 1575 Calle Joaquin, San Luis Obispo.

Santa Lucia Rockhounds
(805) 438-3764
Meets at 7 p.m. the third Monday of each month at Centennial Park, 600 Nickerson Drive, Paso Robles.

Single Moms Social Group
(805) 541-3469
Group catering specifically to the needs of single mothers with school age children and younger.

South County Aquatics
(805) 489-8691

scawaves.usswim.net
A USA Swimming-affiliated competitive swim team serving residents of southern San Luis Obispo County. Swimmers of all abilities ages 5 to 18 are eligible for the program.

Stillehavet Lodge – Sons of Norway
(805) 481-9369
Learn Scandinavian tradition, dance and more with this group of jokesters at 7 p.m. second Fridays, Odd Fellows Hall, 520 Dana St., San Luis Obispo.

Surfrider Foundation, San Luis Bay Chapter
(949) 492-8170
Perhaps known most for its storm-drain stenciling program, this organization promotes clean beaches, surf safety and public beach access.

Toastmasters International, Club 7157
(805) 473-1025
Learn to speak publicly by practicing with the club at 6 p.m. the first and third Tuesdays at Marie Callender's, 2131 Price St., Pismo Beach.

Toastmasters International, Club 5204
(805) 545-8855
www.noontime.org
Learn to speak publicly by practicing with the club from noon to 1 p.m. first and third Tuesdays at First American Title, 899 Pacific St., San Luis Obispo.

Toastmasters International, Cambria
(805) 927-0491
Learn to speak publicly by practicing with the club at 12:15 p.m. first and third Wednesdays, Mid-State Bank & Trust, 1059 Main St., Cambria.

Toastmasters, SLO
(805) 441-3893
Learn to speak publicly by practicing with the club at 6:30 a.m. Thursdays at Odd Fellows Hall, 520 Dana St., San Luis Obispo.

Toastmasters, Speakeasy
(805) 238-3070
Learn to speak publicly by practicing with the club from 12:10 p.m. to 1:15 p.m. Fridays, Paso Robles School District Administration Office, 800 Niblick Road, Paso Robles.

TOO SLO Turtle Club
(805) 481-5222
The local chapter of the California Turtle and Tortoise Club meets at 7 p.m. on second Wednesdays at the PG&E Community Building, 6588 Ontario Road, Avila Valley.

Index

Numbers

Quick! I need another copy!

Best Family Adventures: San Luis Obispo County

Ship to

Name: _____

Address: _____

City: _____ State: _____ ZIP: _____

Telephone (optional): _____

Number of copies _____

Shipping in U.S. ($4 first book, $2/addtl.) _____

Subtotal _____

7.75% tax (if ship to CA address) _____

Total enclosed _____

Mail to: Pen & Pad Publishing, P.O. Box 2995, Orcutt, CA 93457
Questions? (805) 938-1307 or www.bestfamilyadventures.com

Quick! I need another copy!

Best Family Adventures: San Luis Obispo County

Ship to

Name: _____

Address: _____

City: _____ State: _____ ZIP: _____

Telephone (optional): _____

Number of copies _____

Shipping in U.S. ($4 first book, $2/addtl.) _____

Subtotal _____

7.75% tax (if ship to CA address) _____

Total enclosed _____

Mail to: Pen & Pad Publishing, P.O. Box 2995, Orcutt, CA 93457
Questions? (805) 938-1307 or www.bestfamilyadventures.com

Quick! I need another copy!

Best Family Adventures: San Luis Obispo County

Ship to

Name: _____

Address: _____

City: _____ State: _____ ZIP: _____

Telephone (optional): _____

Number of copies _____

Shipping in U.S. ($4 first book, $2/addtl.)_____

Subtotal _____

7.75% tax (if ship to CA address) _____

Total enclosed _____

Mail to: Pen & Pad Publishing, P.O. Box 2995, Orcutt, CA 93457
Questions? (805) 938-1307 or www.bestfamilyadventures.com

Quick! I need another copy!

Best Family Adventures: San Luis Obispo County

Ship to

Name: _____

Address: _____

City: _____ State: _____ ZIP: _____

Telephone (optional): _____

Number of copies _____

Shipping in U.S. ($4 first book, $2/addtl.)_____

Subtotal _____

7.75% tax (if ship to CA address) _____

Total enclosed _____

Mail to: Pen & Pad Publishing, P.O. Box 2995, Orcutt, CA 93457
Questions? (805) 938-1307 or www.bestfamilyadventures.com

Best Suggestions

Pen & Pad Publishing

P.O. Box 2995

Orcutt, CA 93457

Best Suggestions

Pen & Pad Publishing

P.O. Box 2995

Orcutt, CA 93457

HEY! What about *my* favorite place?

If you'd like to share something I missed, please drop me
a note via U.S. mail, or e-mail me at
outdoor411@aol.com

HEY! What about *my* favorite place?

If you'd like to share something I missed, please drop me
a note via U.S. mail, or e-mail me at
outdoor411@aol.com